In memory of Arthur and Vera,
my steadfast, faithful and
unassuming parents

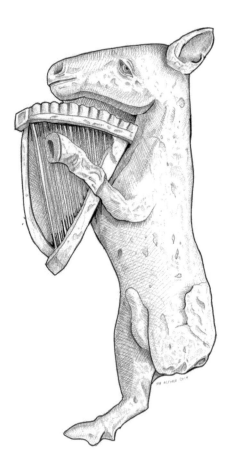

SERIES EDITORS' PREFACE

THE UNIVERSITY OF WALES Press series on Medieval Animals explores the historical and cultural impact of animals in this formative period, with the aim of developing new insights, analysing cultural, social and theological tensions and revealing their remarkable resonances with our contemporary world. The series investigates ideas about animals from the fifth century to the sixteenth, and from all over the world. Medieval thought on animals preserved and incorporated a rich classical inheritance, and some attitudes towards animals that we might consider as having characterized the Middle Ages persisted up to the Enlightenment era – and even to the present day.

When we think about medieval animals, we might variously mean livestock, individual specimens of the genus or species in a particular historical era, or the companion and support to practical human concerns ranging from travel to arable harvests; we might also speak of symbolic creatures and emblems, fictional creatures whose existence is rooted in medieval imagination, the bestiary creature lauded or disparaged for its association with culturally coded behavioural traits, or the animal of natural hierarchy who provides the philosophical and symbolic counterpoint to reason or civilization – the animal as nonhuman. The titles in the series therefore engage with theoretical perspectives and philosophical questions from both the medieval and modern eras, with a concern for intersectional approaches bringing together animality with studies of gender, sexuality, race and postcolonial theory. They build on the diverse and influential reflexes of the 'animal turn' in critical theory and humanities scholarship, encompassing both *animality studies* (on the relation of human and animal in cultural studies) and *animal studies* (with its concomitant considerations for nonhuman advocacy).

A range of different formats has been chosen to reflect the diversity of the medieval primary sources and the wide interdisciplinary academic research they have inspired which will encourage a general readership through pithy, accessible and appealing books. Medieval Animals is the first series to systematically explore the roles and perceptions of individual animals during the Middle Ages. The 'Introducing...' titles focus on the importance of specific animals in art, literature and history; the primary sources reader is designed to support deeper and broader access to evidence encompassing art and architecture, documentary and literary sources, scientific texts and zooarchaeology; finally, longer academic studies engage with and advance the field. The series promotes work that challenges preconceptions, advances the field of study, and engages a wide readership.

Diane Heath and Victoria Blud
Series editors

CONTENTS

ACKNOWLEDGEMENTS

THIS BOOK WOULD not have been possible without various forms of assistance from numerous people and institutions, and I take this opportunity to acknowledge them here. First, a very big thank you to Diane Heath, for inviting me to write this book. I've always had a soft spot for donkeys and writing this book has only increased my admiration and appreciation for them. Thank you to everyone at the University of Wales Press, especially Sarah Lewis and the anonymous reviewers for their support and guidance; and thanks also to the collegial scholars I contacted 'out of the blue' with questions about donkeys, especially Max Harris, Jill Bough and Elvis Mallorquí; likewise, thank you to Mr Alford for his excellent artwork.

At the University of Melbourne, thanks to the School of Historical and Philosophical Studies (SHAPS) and the Baillieu Library. Special thanks to various libraries and archives for access to a range of images: The Morgan Library and Museum; the town of Bayeux; the British Library; the Bibliothèque national de France; and the Library of

Congress. I also acknowledge the financial support of several awards: the University of Melbourne French Trust Fund, the Australian Research Council Associate Investigator Award |2015| (project number CE110001011) and the SHAPS/CHE Research Support Scheme (Centre for the History of Emotions), University of Melbourne. These awards financed a research trip to several European archives, the results of which have informed sections of this book. And finally, a very big thanks to all the people who have travelled on my donkey journey and offered support, encouragement and advice: Jason, Julianna, Kerstin, Holly, Marilyn, and everyone at RIC; your contributions were indispensable.

LIST OF
ILLUSTRATIONS

LIST OF
ABBREVIATIONS

ANZAC   Australian and New Zealand Army Corps

LATCH   *Journal for the Study of the Literary Artifact in Theory, Culture, or History*

NRCF   Willem Noomen and Nico van den Boogaard (eds), *Nouveau Recueil Complet des Fabliaux*, 10 vols (Assen: Van Gorcum, 1983–98) (Noomen and Boogaard were co-editors of volumes 1–5, Noomen was the sole editor of volumes 6–10)

PG   J.-P. Migne (ed.), *Patrologiae Cursus Completus. Series Graeca*, 162 vols (Paris: Garnier, 1857–87)

PL   J.-P. Migne (ed.), *Patrologiae Cursus Completus. Series Latinus*, 222 vols (Paris: Garnier, 1844–1902)

PMLA   *Publications of the Modern Language Association of America*

INTRODUCTION

[The ass] is a sluggish and senseless beast . . .
but is . . . useful and tolerates work,
not complaining even if it is badly neglected.

(Bestiary, Bodleian Library MS, Bodl. 764)

I N A THIRTEENTH-CENTURY image (Illustration 1) we can see an ass whose load is being transferred to a baggage cart. Judging from the amount of goods in the cart and the ass's stooping head and neck, our ass has been busy carrying loads for a considerable time. This image of the ass as a hard-working beast of burden would have been familiar to most people in the Middle Ages. In medieval society, the ass was an unremarkable but indispensable beast: it carried packs, contributed to farm life, and pulled heavy loads. The ass helped the poor and the rich carry out their daily commitments; it accompanied armies on their campaigns, took produce to and from markets, enabled merchants to make deliveries, and carried people to and from their destinations. Yet despite its hard-working reputation, as the image on this book's front cover reveals, the ass was also associated with laziness. The slothful man who is too lazy to pull up his stockings, lethargically rests his head in one hand; he cannot even open his eyes and carries his sword backwards as a symbol of unpreparedness, all whilst riding an ass – the slow-to-react, sluggish beast.

In medieval society then, the ass was a paradox: a beast of contradictory repute. It was at once a mundane, everyday beast and one that, in medieval texts, had an eclectic reputation. The ass was the epitome of folly and obstinacy. Fable asses had a reputation for being stupid, and the bestiary ass was stubborn and slow. Asses also

had a reputation for sexual deviancy. According to some medieval writers, in the natural world, asses who mated with horses to produce mules practised unnatural copulation. One fictitious ass was compelled to have sex with a woman. Asses were also associated with notions of the sacred and the virtuous. Sainte Foy of Conques, a fourth-century child martyr, performed the miracle of resurrection, reviving a dead ass, and in the Old Testament, Balaam's ass delivered God's word through the act of speaking. In the New

Illustration 1: *The War Effort*, *Old Testament Miniatures* (Paris, France, *c.*1244–54), MS M.638, f.27v, The Morgan Library and Museum, New York, USA, purchased by J. P. Morgan (1867–1943) in 1916.

Testament, Christ's decision to ride an ass into Jerusalem on Palm Sunday meant that the lowly beast became associated with the Christian virtues of patience and humility. In the medieval world, the ass's reputation – sacred or profane, derided or acclaimed – was codified in fact, fiction and image. However unusual its binary nature may seem to the modern-day reader, paradoxical rhetoric was a common feature in medieval beast genres, and the fact that the ass had contesting reputations offers multiple avenues for analysis. Even the various names ascribed to the ass are eclectic and contradictory. Often the ass in question would be instantly recognisable as much by its diminutive or pet name as by its Latin name. It was not until the eighteenth century when Carl Linnaeus, the father of modern taxonomy, introduced his binomial nomenclature that the ass was identified by its scientific name – E*quus africanus asinus*.[1]

A*sinus*, *assellus* or onager, Brunellus (sometimes Burnellus) or Carcophas, donkey or ass – these are just some of the medieval and modern names that have been ascribed to the humble beast of burden. Like the ass's reputation they too can be contradictory, with descriptive, ironic and even modest nomenclatures. In the Middle Ages, learned authors used a variety of Latin names to identify the ass: *asinus* ('ass') and *assellus* ('little ass'). Isidore of Seville's etymological assessment associated *asinus* with the Latin verb *sedere* ('to sit') to reinforce the ass's subjugated nature.[2] The wild ass, onager, had a descriptive title whose name was derived from the Greek *on*, meaning 'ass', and *agrios* for 'wild'.[3] It did not inhabit medieval Europe, but it was known by medieval authors and featured in animal compendiums. The onager shared its name with an ancient and early medieval form of catapult. Just as the beastly onager was reputed to use its back legs to kick stones at its hunters, the operative of the onager weapon violently hurled rocks at the enemy, invoking the proverbial image, 'to kick like a mule'.

Literary asses, such as Brunellus and Carcophas, also had descriptive names. The twelfth-century Canterbury monk Nigel Wireker, in his satirical *Speculum Stultorum*, named his ass Brunellus. Wireker derived the ass's name from the Latin *brunus* ('brown'), meaning 'little brown' and whilst this, no doubt, reflected the ass's colouring, it also suggested a dull, unintelligent quality – Wireker's Brunellus to a tee. Another 'brown' literary ass was Burnell, who appeared in the Chester Cycle plays. Rather than implying a dull animal, Burnell was likely an ironic name. In this play, Burnell was the antithesis of its Old Testament owner, Balaam: the metaphorically blind and thus unintelligent prophet, who rode the all-seeing, intelligent ass.[4] There is also conjecture that *donkey*, the modern anglophone word for *ass*, is a similar colour derivative, stemming from the adjective *dun*, to denote the ass's dull greyish-brown colouring.[5]

An even more ironic name from medieval literature is Carcophas, the name of the ass in the twelfth-century Latin beast epic, *Ysengrimus*. Carcophas claims intelligence, explaining:

ego esse magister
Carcophas . . .
Artis ego arridens, Carcophas dicor ab artem
Allatrante Petro, littera totus ego.

> I'm master Carcophas . . . I'm a patron of learning, and
> I'm called Carcophas, from a fusion of 'Cephas' and
> art, with a kind of bark in front of it. I am scholarship
> personified.[6]

In his detailed breakdown, Carcophas demonstrates his
scholarship for Greek and Latin, claiming that his name is
a blend of the two learned worlds although it is prefaced
with an asinine sound. The harsh, bark-like 'C' precedes *ars*,
for 'art and letters', followed by *Cephas*, the Hebrew for Peter
(or the Latin *caput*, for 'head').[7] The author of *Ysengrimus*
brings Carcophas down from his loftiness by making it
clear that Carcophas's name confirms the ass's subjugated,
beast-of-burden nature, stating in a matter-of-fact manner, 'Carcophas the ass, fit for bearing burdens, took his
name from the nature of his duty'.[8] Instead of Carcophas's
self-identifying tripartite etymology, the author relies
simply on the Latin verb *carcare* ('to load/carry a load') to
inform the literary ass's name and nature.

   Even today the ass is known by various names. When
deciding on this book's title, I contemplated 'ass' or 'donkey'. Although English speakers more readily recognise the
ass by its anglicised name – donkey – the medieval world
knew the ass by its Latin name – *asinus*. In the romance
languages of France, Italy, Spain and Portugal, lexically
the Latin tradition has persisted through *l'âne* (*l'asne* –
OF), *asino* and *asno* respectively. In the anglophone world
however, *ass* (beast of burden) is also understood as *arse*
(bottom) depending on the mode of pronunciation. And
it was late eighteenth-century English, with its vary-
ing pronunciations of a long or short 'a', that led to the

introduction of the replacement word 'donkey' to spare any embarrassment to speaker, reader or listener.[9] Eighteenth-century English speakers were merely mirroring the late classical world that also recognised the wordplay of ass and bottom, and often referred to the ass as *asellus*, or even onager, instead of *asinus*. These synonyms were used to avoid the sexual wordplay contained in *asinus*: putting *si* ('yes/sense of the affirmative') into *anus* ('fundament').[10] This then, is a book about donkeys in the medieval world. It is not about arses, bottoms, rears, derrières or behinds, although it will consider the donkey's sensual and sexual appetite, as understood by medieval society.

ORIGINS – NATURE, HOLY, SCHOLASTIC AND LITERARY
Before the ass arrived in medieval Europe, it already had a long association with humankind, and its early history is worth outlining momentarily here as it underpins medieval understandings of this beast. From a natural world perspective, archaeological evidence reveals that humans domesticated the ass around 6,000 years ago in the Middle East, an area often referred to as the Fertile Crescent.[11] Once domesticated, the ass's usefulness as a pack animal facilitated extended trade routes and offered migration possibilities, leading to the geographical spread of people, ideas, goods and the ass across and beyond north Africa and the Middle East. The ancient Greeks brought the ass to the Balkans and the northern shores of the Mediterranean, and the Romans introduced the ass into the rest of continental Europe and the British Isles.

The ancient world ass also held religious and elite significance that predate Christianity, yet inform medieval understandings of the ass. In the Hellenic, Judaic, Roman and other religious traditions of the ancient world, the ass often symbolised sacredness. It also claimed a lofty position in the realm of high priests, kings and gods. In ancient Egypt, asses were ritually immured in royal tomb complexes, carefully oriented eastwards, possibly in response to a sun god and sunrise.[12] In the eighteenth-century BC, the king of Mari, Zimri-Lim, was exhorted to ride an ass as a sign of his kingship. In Damascus, white asses were specially bred for use by the elite class, and Greek and Roman gods rode on the backs of asses.[13] Ancient religious customs conveyed an association between animal, human and deity that influenced medieval religious perspectives of the ass.

In the ancient learned and literary world philosophers and naturalists wrote about the ass in their attempts to explain the natural world, scholars produced practical guides on animal husbandry, and other authors anthropomorphised the ass for entertainment. Aristotle's *Historia Animalium* ('History of Animals', fourth century BC) took a zoological approach to explain the whys and wherefores of animals and their behaviours; Pliny the Elder's *Historia Naturalis* ('Natural History', *c.*AD 79) had an encyclopaedic approach, offering a universal sketch of the ass; Varro's first-century BC *Rerum rusticarum libri tres* ('Three Books on Agriculture') demonstrated the Roman scholar's close knowledge of farming and mule production; and although it was Phaedrus's fables that survived into the medieval period, they were usually credited to Aesop, the ancient Greek slave. Combined, these ancient sources underpinned medieval knowledge of the ass.

THE CHAPTERS

This book engages with scholarship in the fields of animal studies and animality. It considers medieval receptions of the ass and its relation to humans from social and cultural perspectives. Socially, the lived experience of animal–human relations reveals how the ass contributed to human endeavours through its labours; and, conversely, how some humans, especially the medieval encyclopaedists, contributed to knowledge of the ass through forms of proto-zoology. Culturally, the evidence focuses on the animal nature of human beings. Here, the resulting expositions reveal how the ass's varied traits – asinine, irrational, lustful – were projected onto human nature and became tropes and exemplars for human stereotypes and culturally coded behaviours.

Further, the book is thematically organised around four distinct chapters: scientific, religious, scholastic and literary. The chapters provide a survey of the ass through a range of thematic approaches, including didacticism, comedy, gender and emotions. These themes and approaches are not mutually exclusive and, as will become apparent, there is a certain amount of cross-pollination. The ass's natural traits often informed scholastic and literary works – stressing the ass's alleged irrational and foolish nature. Equally, the ass's humble nature derived from Christ's association with the ass also appeared in some literary texts. There are even multiple allusions in medieval ass images. The scene from a sumptuously illustrated thirteenth-century Crusader Bible (Illustration 1) depicts preparations for war by the Old Testament king, David. Here is a picture of an ass in its natural world environment, carrying burdens and doing its daily work. At the same time the ass appears in a religious context. The image of King David's preparations for war was an allegory for preparations for a crusade, with the ass now a participant in a holy war.

Chapter 1, 'The Natural World of the Ass', provides the 'natural science' framework for the ensuing chapters. It opens with an overview of the sources of medieval animal theory that pertains to the ass, especially the medieval encyclopaedic tradition, before moving to an exploration of the ass in the natural and socio-economic world of medieval Europe. Chapter 2, 'The Religious Ass', presents the ass in a variety of religious contexts. Structured around four distinctive themes – the biblical, bestiary, hagiographical and ritual ass, it considers the symbolic and allegorical dimensions of this beast of burden before closing with an assessment of emotional responses to the ass, highlighting the affective process of emotions. This chapter lays the foundations for how medieval people understood the ass through the lens of Christianity and, alongside the 'natural ass', sets up the remaining two chapters. Chapter 3, 'The Scholastic Ass', moves into the realm of the medieval schools. It opens with a consideration of philosophical and scholastic debates on rationality, which often used the ass as a foil for intellect, before closing with a precis of the ass in the scholastic realm of students and masters. Chapter 4, 'The Ass in Literature', investigates the ass's role and function in a variety of medieval literary genres. It is structured around four distinctive themes – the didactic, comedic, political and sexual ass – and concludes with a consideration of the ass's gendered power dynamics and performativity. The final chapter, 'Postscript: The Medieval Ass in the Post-Medieval Era', sums up the evidence and takes a brief look at the ass in a post-medieval context, emphasising continued links to the ass's medieval tropes. This includes the evolving etymology of the ass's name through Shakespeare's 'Bottom' in A *Midsummer Night's Dream*, and associated pejorative terms and phrases, such as jackass, to the infamous line from Quentin Tarantino's 1994 movie, *Pulp Fiction*, 'I'm gonna git [sic] medieval on your ass'.

THE NATURAL
WORLD OF
THE ASS

For there are wonders to be seen in all natural things
(Albertus Magnus, *De animalibus* 11. 86)

I N THE MIDDLE AGES, there were two main ways that
people knew about the ass: either through learned texts
or the commonplace, daily experience. This chapter
focuses on those two perspectives – the theoretical and the
everyday, real world – to provide an overview of the ass in its
natural environment. By the time the ass made an appearance in medieval Europe, its reputation as a slow, stubborn,
senseless but hard-working beast was already well established, and medieval writers recognised four kinds of asses
– domestic (ass), wild (onager), hybrid (mule) and mythical
(onocentaur). The domestic ass, the star of this book, will be
considered in detail in every chapter, whilst the onager, mule
and onocentaur will feature mainly here. Unlike the domestic
ass, the onager did not inhabit medieval Europe, but it
was known through encyclopaedic texts. The mule, a cross
between a male ass and female horse, was a useful animal
in medieval society. Its hybrid vigour made the mule hardier

than the ass: it was able to exist on a poorer diet; it had more
stamina; and it was more sure-footed than its parents. The
thirteenth-century encyclopaedist Thomas of Cantimpré
described the mule as an outstanding animal for its work
abilities. The onocentaur, another hybrid ass, was an exotic
and fantastical beast. A composite, the onocentaur was
described as having either the head of an ass and the body
of a human or vice versa. Its mythical origins likely stem from
a time when non-riding civilisations first saw humans in the
distance riding equids (probably horses).[1] Isidore of Seville
had noted that the horsemen of Thessaly were so adept that
horses and riders seemed to be a single body.[2] Medieval
authors also ascribed to each ass-type distinctive features:
the ass was stubborn but hard-working, the onager was
sensual, the mule was unnatural, and the onocentaur was
both rational and irrational. Some of these idiosyncratic
traits support the evidence for the medieval ass and ass-types
in their lived experiences, but other behaviours and qualities
are consigned to the intellectual world of the erudite.

Illustration 2: Ass *and*
Plough, lower register
of the Bayeux Tapestry,
eleventh century, with
special permission of
the town of Bayeux.

THE THEORETICAL ASS

Encyclopaedias and books of beasts (bestiaries) were the two principal genres from the Middle Ages concerned with delineating the ass. As encyclopaedias were essentially a continuation from the classical world, many medieval authors offered little new information, merely drawing on and incorporating the works of the ancient encyclopaedists, especially Aristotle's *Historia animalium* (fourth century BC) and Pliny the Elder's *Historia naturalis* (*c.*AD 79). Isidore of Seville's *Etymologiae* (AD *c.*625) is one of the earliest medieval encyclopaedias to bridge the gap between the ancient and medieval encyclopaedic traditions. Isidore declared his text a compilation of 'readings from antiquity' that he had read and could recall. It was informed by two approaches: etymological, following the Greek and Hebrew practice to focus on the origins of words to provide meaning, and the Latin encyclopaedic tradition to provide summaries for general learning.[3] Isidore's entry for the ass states:

Asinus et asellus a sedendo dictus, quasi asedus: sed hoc nomen, quod magis equis conveniebat, ideo hoc animal sumpsit quia priusquam equos caperent homines, huic praesidere coeperunt. Animal quippe tardum et nulla ratione renitens, statim ut voluit sibi homo substravit.

The ass (*asinus*) and the 'small ass' (*asellus*, dim. of *asinus*) are so called from 'sitting' (*sedere*), as if the word were *asedus*. The ass took this name, which is better suited to horses, because before people captured horses, they began by domesticating (*praesidere*, lit. 'sit on') the ass. Indeed, it is a slow animal and balks for no reason; it allowed itself to be domesticated as soon as mankind wished it.[4]

As already noted, Isidore's etymology of *asinus* draws attention to the Latin verb *sedere* ('to sit'). He linked *sedere* to domestication via the Latin verb *praesidere*, which also translates as 'to preside (over)', supervise, govern or control, rather than the literal 'to sit on': all imply a sense of subjugation.[5]

After Isidore, a steady stream of medieval encyclopaedic authors dedicated their texts to the natural world, although not all mentioned animals or the ass.[6] By the thirteenth century, animal lore and encyclopaedias had reached an apogee, including Vincent of Beauvais's *Speculum Naturale* in *Speculum Maius* (mid-thirteenth century) and Bartholomeus Anglicus's *De proprietatibus rerum* (1242–7). Medieval authors were especially interested in the human relationship with the natural world, and although medieval encyclopaedias are often considered to have a natural science outlook, it would be imprudent to see this perspective as divorced from a religious perspective. In the Middle Ages, Christian understandings of the world were informed not only by the ancient world encyclopaedic tradition, but also through the Bible, especially the creation story in Genesis. For medieval Christians, God had arranged the natural world in such a way that animals provided lessons for humans by which they should live a morally correct life. Two notable thirteenth-century authors who epitomised this blended approach were Albert the Great (*c*.1200–80) and Thomas of Cantimpré (1201–72). Both were products of the burgeoning scholastic world of the medieval universities. Albert had studied at Padua, Cologne and Paris, whilst Thomas studied under Albert's tutelage in Cologne before completing his studies in Paris. Each became a member of the Dominican Order of Preachers.

Albert's and Thomas's texts, *De animalibus* (1256–68) and *Liber de natura rerum* (1230–45) respectively, illustrate the natural science and religious approaches prevalent in the medieval scholastic milieu. Each text relied heavily on the ancient and patristic *auctores*, including Aristotle, Pliny, the early third century Solinus and Isidore of Seville. As Dominicans, their texts were likely produced for use by university masters and students, as well as by preachers as a means to inform and instruct. Although produced by a master and his student, it was Thomas who produced his *Liber de natura rerum* first, with Albert later copying large sections of Thomas's work into his text, *De animalibus*: clearly their student–teacher relationship had progressed to a point whereby the master had a strong regard for his student's work.[7] Despite being a theologian, master, teacher and eventual Catholic saint, Albert the Great also brought an approach to his work on animals that was more scientific than theological, and that arguably made him a remarkable medieval thinker of science.[8] Unlike some of his contemporaries, he considered the principles of science to be composed of experiment, observation and reflection, and he offered a medical appraisal of the ass grounded in Galenic principles.[9] However, Thomas was more traditional for his time and located his exposition of the ass within a biblical setting, and Thomas's text would influence later works on animals; it was not yet possible to divorce the natural and religious worlds.[10]

Albert and Thomas each considered the ass to be an ugly animal. They described it as having a large head, long, wide ears and a lean body – although Thomas stated that the young ass was 'rather beautiful', only becoming uglier as it aged. Despite the ass's apparent ugliness, each ironically noted the ass's quality to beautify humans, recalling Pliny's account that Nero's mistress, Poppaea, had bathed in ass milk to take advantage of its skin-whitening properties. Albert's humoral approach led him to note the ass's dryness and melancholy. According to him, dryness, combined with earthiness and coldness, formed the basis of the ass's stubborn nature, as it was these features that rendered the animal insensitive to blows and thus difficult to teach. The ass's melancholy formed the basis of its ability to carry heavy loads, as melancholy was focused in its strong, dry bones, found towards its rear. Albert stated that the ass carried burdens better over its kidneys than on its back or shoulders, and this is epitomised in the image on this book's front cover, where the lazy man sits on the hindquarters to ride the ass.[11] Albert also enumerated a range of medicinal and useful properties of the ass – dung, liver, hooves, marrow, urine – which, depending on illness and preparation, could be ingested, applied topically, or used as a fumigant. For instance, to rid a house infested with vermin, Albert recommended using the burnt lungs of an ass to smoke out the house.

Conversely, Thomas located his assessment of the ass within a Christian paradigm. He noted the ass's Christ-like meek and patient nature and equated the cross on the ass's shoulders with the mark of Christ, stating 'in humeris stigmata Christi portat crucis' ('on its shoulders it carries the marks of Christ's cross').[12] Thomas applied accepted ass traits – faithful, stubborn, slow – to make clear distinctions between good and evil acts, sometimes linking the trait to a biblical verse. For instance, in his consideration of the female ass's loyalty and faithfulness to its young, Thomas stated that the ass would pass through fire for its foal. He explained through quoting Christ's words, 'greater love hath no man than this, that a man lay down his life for his friends' (John 15: 13), contrasting the faithfulness of the ass with the evilness of some slothful prelates who would not endure sufferance on their flock's behalf.[13] Through Christ's words, Thomas juxtaposed the ass and the priest to show that a dumb beast was a better exemplar than some Christians when it came to selfless love and charity.

However, Thomas was not unique in relying on Christian interpretation to inform his work on animals. First appearing in the tenth century, a new genre of animal text – the bestiary or book of beasts – achieved the height of its popularity in the thirteenth century. These texts were exegetical in their approach: animals were divine symbols to be understood through allegorical interpretation and their purpose was to allow humans, particularly monks, to know themselves, using animals as a pretext.[14] The bestiary took its inspiration from the *Physiologus*, an anonymous Greek text (mid- to late third century AD), and is considered one of the earliest exegetical sources.[15] Produced in Egypt, the *Physiologus* combined the encyclopaedic tradition with moralising tales that exemplified Christian dogma and allegorical meanings. Already translated into Latin by the fifth century, in the twelfth and thirteenth centuries it had been enlarged, translated, modified, and even versified.[16] Initially a text used almost exclusively within the cloister, with the rise of urban centres and increasing secular spheres of influence, such as the economy and government, the *Physiologus*'s didactic impact spread to the laity. Always a textbook for early learning – reading and writing – the exegetical text shaped the development of the Second-family bestiaries. Read by the laity, the Second-family bestiaries formed part of the Church's *cura pastoralis* (pastoral care) reforms, evident in the decrees of Lateran III and IV, and aimed at meeting the laity's social and spiritual needs: literacy and salvation.[17] The *Physiologus* and the bestiaries now provided moral and spiritual education for religious and laity.

Each animal entry in the *Physiologus* had a tripartite structure, opening with a biblical verse before offering an assessment of the animal's nature and spiritual significance. The following entry is for the wild ass:

> It is said in Job, 'Who has let the wild ass go free?' (Job 39: 5). Physiologus says of the wild ass that being first among those of the herd, if he begets colts, the father will break their necessaries [testicles] so that they produce no seed.

> The patriarchs tried to create carnal seed, but the apostles spiritually obtained carnal sons so that they might possess heavenly seed, just as it is said, 'Rejoice, barren woman who does not bear,' . . . (Is. 54: 1). The Old Testament announces the seed, but the New [Testament] proclaims abstinence.[18]

The opening biblical verse served to introduce the wild ass and presages the tone to follow: obedience and submission to authority (God). The remaining sections used reproduction as a metaphor to justify man's submission. First was a consideration of the wild ass's nature: the jealous male ensured his primacy over the herd by castrating young males. This was followed by a section that allegorised the wild ass as representative of the Old Testament patriarchs and their desire to reproduce in the earthly world; it contrasted with the New Testament's apostles, who were upheld as the exemplar for preaching continence. As the *Physiologus* had noted and later bestiaries maintained, not only did jealous male onagers castrate newborn colts, but the mother onagers gave birth in secret to protect their colts. Within the cloistered monasteries, the wild ass came to be a figure for the celibate monk protected by his mother – the Church.

Through the *Physiologus*'s profound influence on the production of bestiaries, bestiary authors continued to record the natural world attributes of the beasts but also applied a fourfold allegory of biblical exegesis: literal, allegorical, moral and spiritual.[19] Chapter 2 will consider the moral and spiritual interpretations of the bestiary ass but it is worth remarking here that the bestiaries concurred with the encyclopaedias on the ass's natural world attributes.

According to the bestiaries, the ass was a sluggish and sense-less beast, easily subjugated and thus suited to heavy work. Latin bestiaries declared that the ass was a 'tardy beast' ('animal . . . tardum') with 'no reasoning' ('nulla ratione'), that it did not resist man's wish to dominate it ('nulla . . . renitens statim ut voluit sibi homo substravit') and that it 'endures work and neglect' ('laborem tolerat et negligentiam').[20] Twelfth- and thirteenth-century authors evidently recognised the utility of the ass in supporting human endeavours.

A recurring theme associated with the ass was its sexual nature – real and imagined. Whilst the *Physiologus* interpreted the wild ass's reproductive traits morally and mystically, the encyclopaedias took a more pragmatic approach to the ass's alleged sexual and sensual nature, albeit still often within a discernible Christian paradigm. Male and female asses were considered sensual, lustful and carnal. Like the *Physiologus*, in the encyclopaedic and bestiary traditions, the sexual attributes of the ass were often associated with the act of reproduction. Albert and Thomas each noted the ass's birthing habits in that the female avoided light, preferring to give birth in the dark. Albert suggested that this practice could be due to the weakness of the foal's eyes, but Thomas was more assured in his assessment. He linked the birthing process to the New Testament verse, 'Let not thy left hand know what thy right hand doeth' (Matthew 6: 3). Part of Jesus's teach-ings on the benefits of doing good deeds in secret without the need to be boastful, this verse can be understood as emphasising the humble nature of the ass.

Reproductively, the ass also defied the laws of nature as understood in the medieval world, in that it could breed with a horse to produce a mule. Medieval society recognised the mule's hybrid vigour as a positive result of the cross-breeding union, despite its resulting sterility. Thomas declared it an exceptional worker – 'viribus in labore eximium' ('excellent strength regarding toil').[21] Yet, in the learned world, the mule was the result of an unnatural union and attempts to explain it crossed scientific, anthropomorphic and moral boundaries. Thomas of Cantimpré first applied his overarching Christian paradigm to explain the mule in human and moral terms: as the result of an adulterous union, it was conceived evilly and contrary to nature. Then, like Albert, he explained the union via humoral theory, hypothesising that the mule's sterility was based on the opposing constitutions of the parents – the incompatibility of the ass's coldness and the horse's heat. Albert went even further, linking human and mule infertility via sympathetic magic – a type of magic based on imitation or correspondence where, for instance, animal traits could be absorbed by eating or wearing parts of them. He declared that if two mule testicles were hung around a woman's neck she would be as infertile as a mule for as long as she wore them.[22] Despite the mule's hardiness, cross-breeding was an aberration to be explained in negative terms and its sterility became a motif to be applied to the human condition.

As for the ass's sensual, especially carnal, nature, in *De animalibus* Albert informed his readers that during the mating period the ass will be 'aroused most fervently' and will 'act as if crazy, especially if the (mature) ass is a virgin'.[23] Thomas described female onagers similarly; they were highly lustful and unrestrained, behaviour that the male onager apparently found tiresome. Thomas identified the sensual nature of the ass as part of the animal's evil nature. He considered the onager's behaviour as symbolic of men and women, declaring that men hate their unchaste wives as it is contrary to their nature to behave so wantonly: women should be modest. Male onagers were also depicted in lustful terms. Thomas and Albert agreed that a male onager, full of lust but without a partner, would stand atop a mountain and, 'burning with sexual desire', deeply breathe in the cooling air to temper his sexual thirst. As for the onocentaur, bestiaries claimed that it was a symbol of male lust in that the mythical beast's lower monstrous half represented man's animal nature, as opposed to its rational (human) upper half. The third-century philosopher Aelian even considered the beast to be the result of intercourse between two species – a man and an ox or a man and a mare. Although some later medieval commentators rejected this idea, Thomas of Cantimpré was not confident enough to totally reject the notion and as a result confirmed the belief in cross-species breeding, even humans with animals. Using Saint Jerome as an *auctor*, Thomas declared that Jerome had been unsure whether the onocentaur had been formed by humans or the Devil, before continuing that some societies in the East believed in the creature and that it was worthy of worship.[24] The sexual proclivities of the various ass-types informed other understandings of the ass, and the sexual ass is a theme which recurs in later chapters. The encyclopaedias and bestiaries informed and promoted the ass's reputation for sexual promiscuity: any animal that willingly mated with another species must surely be immoral, licentious and uninhibited. Ultimately, the ass's sexual nature highlighted humanity's sexual weaknesses.

Medieval authors made assertions and declarations about the ass that were grounded in duality. Informed by the ancient world *auctores* and the Christian milieu, the result was a dichotomous ass. It was ugly but could beautify; it was melancholic, but its constituent parts could heal; it was a sexual beast that could produce stronger hybrid offspring, but only via unnatural sex; and its Christian allegorisation offered moral instruction. Considering these learned theories, what then was the human–ass experience in the everyday world?

THE ASS'S LIVED EXPERIENCE IN MEDIEVAL EUROPE

Learned authors might have labelled the ass as stubborn, but its ability to carry heavy loads and sure-footedness meant that it was an indispensable beast in everyday situations. One of the earliest medieval accounts attesting to the dissemination of the ass across western Europe was an eighth-century Bavarian law code that outlined work restrictions on the ass. The code proscribed work on a Sunday, paraphrasing Exodus 20: 10, 'No work shall you do on the holy day, neither you . . . nor your ass nor any other which is subject to you.' Yet, unlike other animals mentioned in the codex, the ass was not mentioned elsewhere in the statutes, suggesting that whilst the Bible provided an authority for the legal code, asses were not routinely used in that province at that time.[25] Nonetheless, a contemporary source does reveal isolated evidence for asses in the region, as St Sturm (*c*.705–99) founded a monastery at Fulda after he conducted a search, on the back of an ass, for a suitable monastic site.[26]

In *De animalibus*, Albert the Great noted that the ass rarely thrived above fifty degrees latitude as it was not partial to cold climates – this is approximately north of the English Channel and includes the British Isles and the northern regions of continental Europe. His statement was somewhat upheld in the physical evidence and textual sources, although the ass was not totally absent from northern Europe. The English evidence offers an intriguing case study. The singular remains of a partial ass skeleton (dated eighth–ninth century) provide physical evidence for one ass in Anglo-Saxon England (450–1066); yet its singularity and location – Westminster – next to London's major trade and transport route, the river Thames, cautions against extrapolating one skeleton into evidence for the ass throughout early medieval England.[27] Ass numbers from the post-Norman conquest era (1066) further complicate the picture. William the Conqueror's Domesday Book (1086) – an inventory of settlements, people and their possessions – reveals that asses (and mules) made up a mere 3.9 per cent of working equids in Norman England and Wales (1066–1135); and by the twelfth and thirteenth centuries ass numbers were less than 1 per cent of working equids in the British Isles. Another Norman source, the Bayeux Tapestry (*c.*1170s), further complicates our knowledge of the ass and its purpose in medieval England. The tapestry depicts a single ass drawing a plough in the margins of the embroidery (Illustration 2). This image, however, is problematic, and we need to apply caution before asserting it as representative of actual agricultural practices. Ploughs were usually drawn by teams of animals, and the Domesday record refers only to plough-teams of oxen.

Further confusing the picture of the medieval ass in England is a twelfth-century charter for an abbey at Burton-upon-Trent that lists three Spanish asses in its inventory.

Their actual purpose is not clear, with conflicting schools of thought declaring the asses to be either pack or stud animals.[28] Considering the ass was not the preferred pack animal in England at this time, and as the establishment also contained stud horses, we should give credit to the theory that this demesne farm could very well have bred mules. Two problems arise, however, in confirming this theory. The first is the problem of identification, thanks to the ambiguous terminology used in the sources to define various equids: peasant stock was excluded from the Domesday record and asses were often grouped collectively under a catch-all category that also included mules.[29] The second is the unreliability of extrapolating the stud practice to other English estates; ass and mule numbers for England remained sparse throughout the later medieval centuries. A further line of enquiry that the presence of the Spanish asses raises, and is yet to be addressed in the scholarship, concerns the ass's economic value as a stud animal and the investment in trading livestock during this period: was it a restricted monastic activity, or did other non-religious estates practise ass breeding? Who were the merchants facilitating livestock trade into England: English, Spanish, secular, religious? And who was riding the beasts?

There are two opposing conclusions that we can draw from the English evidence: one, that in 1086, when the Domesday records were made, the ass may have been either a vestige of the Roman Empire or an Anglo-Saxon tradition, but one that diminished with increasing Norman influences; or two, that after the fall of the Roman Empire, the ass in England virtually disappeared and was reintroduced at the time of the Norman Conquest, from when its numbers slowly increased. Asses certainly had a presence in northern France from the seventh century onwards, which offers support to the latter theory that they might very well have been introduced to England via the Normans.[30] The limited numbers in England might also indicate their restricted use by a small group of society; in the Middle Ages, clerics rode asses (and mules) due to the animal's association with Christ.

Below the fiftieth latitude, however, the available evidence certainly points to the ubiquity of the ass. Because the ass was mostly associated with the poorest members of society, it was less likely to appear in official records and we must rely on vestigial evidence from the period – archaeological, material, as well as official and personal records – to build a picture of the ass and its uses. For instance, archaeological evidence from a late eleventh- to early twelfth-century fortified settlement in the Dordogne unsurprisingly attests to the presence of more asses in the village than the castle.[31] Records from ninth-century Provence, where land usage in rocky uplands was described as 'colonica as asinarum' ('ass pasture'), attest to their sure-footedness and suitability for precarious terrain.[32] And in fourteenth-century Catalonia, many manorial farms in the diocese of Girona were recorded as having one ass but multiple oxen, supporting the notion that here the ass was used as a pack, rather than draught, animal.[33] Asses were put to work in monastic houses, small farms and mills, where they would turn the grinding stones.[34] They were used as pack animals, in one source recorded as transporting goods from northern France to Marseille for further transportation across the Mediterranean.[35] No doubt their sure-footedness, which the animal treatises hint at through the ass's caution at crossing slatted bridges, would have been providential for the mountain passes that had to be negotiated on the southward journey through France.[36]

Some regions offer evidence of asses and mules being shod, further supporting their use as a pack animal carrying loads and people over hard and rocky terrain. In England, whilst there are records attesting to the universality of horse-shoeing practices, only a small number of mule shoes have been cautiously identified, from a medieval archaeological site in London.[37] This is, of course, in keeping with the limited ass and mule presence at this time in the British Isles. In other regions however, the evidence is more striking. At the fortified settlement of Andone, in the Charente region of France, ass, horse and mule shoes, as well as a large range of tools associated with shoeing, reveal active blacksmithing and farrier practices dating from the eleventh century.

In death, the ass continued to provide for its human masters. Excavations of southern French tanneries reveal the practice of skinning asses after death to turn their hides into leather.[38] Albert the Great noted ass leather that originated from where the beast had carried its burdens in life was extremely tough. He recounted that his own shoes made from ass leather were most durable and suitable for continued walking over rocky terrain: although he did declare that prolonged use of the shoes had led to the leather becoming too tough to wear.[39] It seems also that ass meat might have been too tough, as it was not routinely consumed during the Middle Ages. Hildegard of Bingen stated that it was not good to eat the ass's flesh, as it was 'fetid from . . . [its] stupidity'.[40] Here she clearly associated the ass's nature with its inability to nourish humans. Regardless of Hildegard's opinion, Christian prohibitions on the consumption of equids followed Judaic dietary practices. Pope Gregory III banned hippophagy – the consumption of horse flesh – in 732; his decree was actually aimed at prohibiting pagan traditions in newly Christianised lands. However, in some places long-standing local traditions appear to have superseded Christian canonical law. Across the Middle Ages, communities in sporadic locations do appear to have routinely consumed ass meat.[41]

Consumption of ass meat was predominantly associated with peasant populations, but exceptions occurred, mainly in times of crisis. In the early fifteenth century, at a site on the frontier between the Muslim kingdom of Granada and the Christian kingdom of Castile, evidence points to a greater ass consumption than at any other time in the region's history. A combined archaeological and historical assessment suggests a period of border conflict and heightened political and economic crisis resulted in an increased population – military and refugee – that stressed the available food resources to the point where people resorted to ass meat out of necessity rather than choice.[42] This was not an isolated incident; it had been a similar story during the First Crusade. Many eyewitness and contemporary accounts record the crusaders eating asses. The *Gesta Francorum* ('Deeds of the Franks') detailed that people ate their asses – 'asinos nostros manducaremus' ('we were eating our asses') – when they were under siege and out of provisions, and Fulcher of Chartres highlighted the crusaders' desperation: 'dying from hunger . . . our men killed our famished . . . asses, and ate them'.[43] Peter Tudebode noted that crusaders even boiled old hides of asses (and other animals) to extract nourishment from the liquid, such were their hardships 'suffered in the name of Christ'.[44] Tales of eating ass meat even made it to crusade literature, signalling its practice as exceptional and a sign of desperation.[45] The overriding sentiment from the crusade sources is that not only were the crusaders at the point of starvation that they would eat an ass, but that crusading nobles were reduced to the same level as peasants.

However unfamiliar the crusaders were with eating ass meat, there can be little doubt that they would have appreciated its nutritional value – eyewitness accounts tell of the crusaders resorting to anything that might sustain them: shoe leather, thistles, even, according to the chronicler Fulcher of Chartres, 'the seeds of grain found in manure'.[46] The value of the asses who gave their lives for the crusaders is immeasurable, and estimating medieval ass values in more tangible terms, especially fiscal, is equally difficult, thanks to the fragmentary records. Nonetheless, it is possible to make some estimation as to their value. The ox may have been preferred as a draught animal to pull the plough – it was cheaper to feed than the ass – but in the very early medieval period some of the poorest of farmers may have used asses, confirming their low monetary value.[47] Yet many medieval societies developed hierarchies when placing a value on animals, based on their worth to an individual or community. Animals associated with the elite classes attracted the highest value. These were followed by animals that laboured, with animals that were raised for food holding the least value.[48] Although there is no direct evidence for the value of an ass, we could deduce that the ass would likely attract a value commensurate with the labouring animals. As laws were instituted by the elites it should come as no surprise to see that animals associated with the noble pursuits of war and hunting attracted the highest value; in early medieval Germanic law codes, the value of a war horse was four times higher than that of a draught horse.[49] During the first crusade the low social standing of the ass was epitomised in Albert of Aachen's statement that many eminent men acquired asses and used them as horses, even princes:

> Ex hiis vero egregiis viris qui mulum aut assellum vel vile iumentum vel palefridum nunc adquirere poterat pro equo utebatur. Inter quos fortissimo et ditissimi sua in terra principes asino insidentes certamen inierunt.

> Any of these eminent men who had now been able to acquire a mule or a donkey or a worthless pack animal or a palfrey used it as a horse. Among them, princes who were very powerful and rich in their own land went into battle riding on a donkey.[50]

Albert implies the exceptional nature of the situation in that an ass did not befit a prince; yet desperate times called for desperate measures, and princes were not too proud to sit upon an ass, or to beg for the use of one.[51] For those who did have money during the difficult periods of the First Crusade, an ass could command an overinflated price. During the siege at Antioch, when the crusaders were without food, the local population exploited the situation to their advantage, and crusaders paid one bezant for an ass's head and ten shilling for its entrails: 'pro capite unius asini . . . bisantius unus dabatur and in uisceribus . . . decem solidi' ('for the head of an ass . . . was paid one bezant and for entrails . . . ten solidus [gold coins]').[52] The author makes it clear that these prices were out of the ordinary. Societies that did not apply strict hierarchies to animal usage equally did not discriminate between values of similar animals used for different tasks – such as between war and cart horses.[53] In eleventh-century Catalonia (1064), leading bishops and princes adopted and confirmed the Truce of God treaty, proscribing the plunder of beasts, including male and female asses, thus protecting the peasantry from undue attack and hardship and placing an economic value on the ass.[54]

The ass's value can also be estimated in social terms as well as fiscally. Religious men rode asses and mules as a sign of asceticism. The sixth-century bishop Gregory of Tours noted the austerity of an oblate who rode an ass as a sign of self-restraint. Gregory likened this act to eating barley instead of wheat, or drinking water as a substitute for wine. Peter the Hermit also rode an ass whilst preaching the First Crusade (1095).[55] Pious bequests in wills and testaments also confirm the association between ass and priest; a late eleventh-century Catalonian will revealed that a small landholder left an ass, amongst other modest bequests, to a local monastery.[56]

The medieval ass was a utilitarian beast that assisted people in their daily endeavours. Although not suited to the more northerly, cooler regions of Europe, its distribution was widespread in the warmer regions, where it worked tirelessly. Scholars may have theorised about the ass, but they rarely engaged with the realities of this beast of burden, and their more fanciful imaginings of the ass only persisted in works of fiction.

THE RELIGIOUS
ASS

Rejoice greatly, O daughter of Zion; shout, O daughter
    Jerusalem:
Behold, thy king cometh unto thee: he is just and having
    salvation;
Lowly, and riding upon an ass, and upon a colt, the foal
    of an ass.

(Zechariah 9: 9)

And Jesus, when he had found a young ass, sat thereon;
    as it is written,
Fear not, daughter of Sion: behold, thy King cometh,
    sitting on an ass's colt.

(John 12: 14–15)

THIS CHAPTER FOCUSES on the medieval ass in
its religious environment and reflects the cultural
integration of Christianity across every sphere of
social and political life in western Europe. As we saw in the
beast texts from chapter 1, animals were part of God's creation, and the medieval Church placed great significance
on the ways in which animals could provide lessons on
Christian morality and show the way to humanity's eternal
salvation. In the case of the ass, symbolic and allegorical
representations dominated the exegesis. Medieval authors
found multiple ways to interpret the ass, which resulted in

a heterogeneous religious ass; it could be holy and humble as well as stubborn and foolish. This chapter showcases the mutable ass from four Christian perspectives: that of the bible, the bestiaries, hagiographies and holy days, theorising the ass from a history of emotions perspective.

THE BIBLICAL ASS

As the pre-eminent Christian text, the Bible provided the foundation for the ass's association with holy matters. Biblical asses appear throughout the text, at pivotal and more liminal moments. Their presence not only reinforced the perception of the ass's natural traits but also offered the opportunity to bestow an exegetical role on the ass. In the New Testament, the ass featured at seminal points in Christ's life: it carried a pregnant Mary to Jerusalem; alongside the ox, it adored the infant Christ in the stable – 'bos et asinum adorabant' ('the ox and ass adored [him]'); it carried the Holy Family in their flight to Egypt, to escape Herod's Massacre of the Innocents; and on Palm Sunday, the adult Christ made a triumphal entry into Jerusalem riding an ass.[1] That the ass participated at key moments in the life of Christ points to its symbolic and ceremonial role as the bearer of salvation.

Christ's association with the ass had its origins in the Old Testament, where certain events were claimed to presage Christ's life. The opening epigraph highlights one of the most well-known examples: Christ's triumphal entry into Jerusalem on Palm Sunday, as described in the gospels and prophesied in Zechariah 9: 9.[2] The ass also played a role in another Old Testament prophecy (Genesis 22: 1–14). When Abraham and his son Isaac journeyed to the

Mount in Moriah to sacrifice Isaac at God's bidding, Isaac travelled on the back of an ass. At the moment of sacrifice God intervened; Isaac was saved and replaced by a ram. Early Christian writers, including Hippolytus of Rome (*c*.170–235) and Origen (*c*.184–*c*.253), considered this event to prefigure God's plan to have His own Son, Christ, sacrificed in atonement for the sins of the world. Although the ass played a liminal role in this story, the lowly beast served as the bearer of salvation, carrying Isaac – the precursor of Christ.

Other ass appearances in the Old Testament corroborated the ass's natural attributes – its sturdy, hard-working reputation and ability to carry heavy loads. Moses had an ass carry his wife and child across the desert to Egypt in his attempt to free any remaining Israelites from the Pharaoh's rule (Exodus 4: 18–20): and laden asses carried loads of corn from Egypt during a time of famine (Genesis 42: 26).[3] The biblical ass also combined its practical attributes with figurative meanings. Asses functioned as symbols of peace, such as when the virtuous Abigail sent food to David and his army in a successful bid to prevent war; she rode an ass and the food was carried on a caravan of asses (1 Samuel 25: 14–35).

Besides signifying peace, medieval authors offered other figurative meanings for the beast of burden. In the New Testament, that the ass was closely associated with the life of Christ pointed to its submissive, obedient and humble disposition. Jesus rode an unbroken ass, sending two of His disciples to fetch it, saying: 'Go your way into the village over against you: . . . ye shall find a colt tied, whereon never man sat. Loose him and bring him'

(Mark 11: 2). A literal reading of this verse demonstrates how the ass was an easily subjugated beast. Metaphorically, the unridden ass represented a people (humankind) yet to become submissive to a higher authority. The ass, like good Christians, willingly submitted to Christ and from its servile and obedient nature, the medieval ass became associated with the virtue of humility – 'ce est la beste d'umilité' ('it is the beast of humility').[4]

The ass's humble nature also warrants attention as another potential paradox. Although many medieval writers associated Christ's choice of an ass to ride into Jerusalem as a sign of humility, paradoxically, and especially in pre-Christian eras, asses were a sign of status reserved for the elite – judges, priests and kings. The Old and New Testaments epitomise the ass as an elite mount. The book of Judges declares: 'Speak, ye that ride on white asses, ye that sit in judgment' (Judges 5: 10), whilst the four gospels that recount Christ's triumphal Palm Sunday entry into Jerusalem also reinforce the privileged status of the ass. Matthew, Luke and John each expressly recognise Jesus as a king, whilst Mark styles the people's reaction to His arrival as the adoration of the Messiah through their shouts of 'Hosanna' – 'saviour'. In contrast to warmongering kings, who rode horses, kings who rode asses signified that they were riding in peace, like the Old Testament king Solomon, who deliberately rode an ass as a sign of peace. The biblical implication was that the meek Christ rode a humble ass into Jerusalem to signify that He had come in peace, as a king of spiritual force for spiritual ends. Christ may have been humble, riding a lowly ass, but He was still a king, riding a king's mount.

The most dynamic biblical ass would have to be Balaam's Old Testament ass (Numbers 22: 22–35). One of only two biblical animals to have the power of speech, this ass ensured that its master obeyed God's will and was the antithesis of the Bible's other speaking animal, the Garden of Eden's evil serpent. Whilst the ass was carrying Balaam towards his God-forbidden task, an angel wielding a sword blocked their path three times. The ass saw God's messenger and changed course three times to avoid destruction; Balaam could not see the angel and thrice beat his ass, believing it to have stubbornly refused to obey him. At this point, God gave the ass the power of speech, putting words in its mouth; it questioned why Balaam had beaten it despite its long and loyal service (Numbers 22: 28–30). It was only at this point that Balaam recognised the significance of the ass's actions, saw the angel, and submitted to God's will.

The sculpted Romanesque capital (*c.*1120) in the church of Saint-Andoche, Saulieu (Illustration 3) depicts the moment in Numbers when the ass, confronted by the sword-wielding angel, abruptly came to a halt and turned away from the heavenly messenger. In this masterpiece of stonework, the sculptor vividly captured the ass's startled look, and when viewed from below Balaam is leaning slightly towards the viewer, as if he is about to fall off his mount. The mason took full advantage of the capital's shape to effectively depict the narrative and highlight the juxtaposition of sight and knowledge. As Balaam and the angel are at right angles to each other, only the ass, whose head slightly protrudes around the capital corner, can see the angel. Not only can the viewer see that Balaam

Illustration 3: *Balaam's Ass sees the Angel*, based on the capital at the church of Saint-Andoche, Saulieu, France. Illustration by Mr Alford.

is literally blind to the angel's presence, but medieval Christians would have recognised Balaam's metaphorical blindness.

There are several ways to understand Balaam's talking ass. Its natural propensity and reputation for stubbornness provided the foundation for the tale. On this rudimentary level, we are not surprised to learn of the ass's disobedience. More critical interrogation reveals the ass as a didactic beast; not only does it teach its master the importance of obeying God, it serves as an exemplar for Christians to emulate. A traditionally senseless, stubborn beast, Balaam's ass was a model for obedience, whose behaviour was sanctioned by God through the power of divinely given speech. Equally then, Christians of all social classes and abilities could follow the ass's obedient example. Another, more comic, reading of Balaam's ass focuses on the thematic motifs of sight and vision. Balaam, the blind prophet or (un)seer, contrasts sharply with the visual acumen of his ass. Although perceived as a comedic event, it remains a didactic moment – learning through laughter – teaching the wilfully blind about the nature of God's wrath and the lesson of obedience.[5]

For early Christian exegetes, Balaam and his ass were paradoxical. In his homilies on the Book of Numbers, Origen took an allegorical approach to understand the meaning of Balaam and his ass. For him, Balaam represented the Jewish elites – Pharisees and scribes – and riding the subjugated ass was representative of the oppressed ordinary people: '[S]cribae autem et Pharisaei errant qui sedebant super asinam hanc, et tenebant eam vinctam' ('Scribes and Pharisees err who sit upon the ass thus, and keep them [the people] restrained').[6] However, Balaam's paradox is that he was at once a prophet who foretold the Incarnation (Numbers 24: 17) and an agent of the Israelite's idolatry (Numbers 25 and 31: 16). Origen used Balaam's ass – the innately contradictory animal – to explain the prophet's conflicting natures: where the ass once carried false belief (Balaam), it now carries Christ: 'haec asina, id est ecclesia, prius portabat Balaam, nunc autem Christum' ('this ass, that is the church, previously was carrying Balaam, now however, it carries Christ').[7] In this way, Origen explained the ass as the two monotheistic faiths – the old Judaic and the new Christian. Origen's twofold explanation hinted at an underlying prejudice that favoured the Christian faith over Judaism, and this partiality recurred in later medieval texts, particularly the bestiaries.

THE BESTIARY ASS

As chapter 1 has already dealt with the bestiary ass as a literal beast, here I will focus on the allegorical, moral and spiritual interpretations of the ass. Morally, bestiary animals and their behaviours served as reflections of the human world. Animals symbolised human qualities or faults, offering bestiary readers the opportunity to apply the oppositional vice–virtue cycle to animals.[8] Bestiary authors used animals to stress the many vices, including pride, lust and avarice, which might befall sinners, and the desirable virtues to which they should aspire in their quest for salvation, such as humility, chastity and largesse. Spiritually, animal interpretations in the bestiaries relied on scriptural authority to inform, and the animal kingdom offered simultaneous representations of good and evil. Often, spiritual readings were not restricted to the Christian world's opposing forces of good and evil, God and the Devil, but also stepped into non-Christian worlds; for instance, some interpretations of animals relied on oppositional faiths, such as Judaism and Christianity, to deliver spiritual lessons as Christian authors sought to defend their faith as the rightful inheritors of the mantle of God's chosen people.[9] For medieval readers, the moral and spiritual constructs of the bestiary ass were opportunities to show Christians, and non-believers, the only way to salvation.

Taking the *Physiologus* as a template, many medieval bestiaries tended to feature the wild, rather than domestic, ass. Possibly because of its untamed, wandering nature, the bestiary wild ass (onager) offered an almost universal spiritual reading as a representative of the Devil; paradoxically, the exception was when the onager represented the monk. Notwithstanding this, and as was typical of most bestiaries, Guillaume, the Norman clerk's *Bestiaire Divin* (*c*.1210) stated that the wild ass was 'le symbole du Malin' ('the symbol of the Evil One').[10] Bestiary authors fused two features from the *Physiologus* – repeated braying and the vernal equinox – to present the wild ass as a symbol for the hungry Devil (Job 6: 5). The exegetical interpretation propounded that as the spring equinox signalled the shortening of the hours of darkness, the Devil had fewer opportunities to seek out nourishment – sinners. This equinox also indicated the impending Pasch (first Sunday after the full moon, post-equinox) that lessened the numbers of sinners as they re-committed to God in paschal observances. The vernal equinox and ensuing Pasch resulted in fewer sinners to satiate the Devil's hunger and he was compelled to cry out incessantly, like a hungry wild ass braying relentlessly. An inverse reading of the same scenario located the ass's constant braying within the cloister. Monks, the original bestiary audience, understood themselves as onagers. The bestiary led the religious to comprehend the onager's braying in the desert at the vernal equinox, as the tolling of a church bell alerting monks to the call and safety of the Church: just as the onager marked the equinox by braying every hour, so, too, did the monks observe the hours through prayer.

In the vice–virtue cycle, hunger could also be interpreted as a sexual hunger and morally the ass cautioned against lust and lechery. Here, bestiary authors relied heavily on the ass's natural traits. The scribe of the English bestiary Bodley 764 (*c*.1225–50) invoked the ass's sensual as well as irrational and placid nature, stating that the ass's name implied 'lecherous' (*libidinorum*), 'gentle' (*mansuetudo*) and 'foolish' (*stultitia*).[11] The same scribe introduced a series of Old Testament verses that mentioned the ass to caution the reader against various vices. To underscore the relationship between the ass and a foolish man, Bodley 764 presented the example of the Patriarch Jacob, who censured his son's slothfulness, lamenting: 'Issachar is a strong ass, couching down between two burdens' (Genesis 49: 14). Rather than using his strength to work hard like an ass, Issachar eschewed a life of toil in favour of worldly pleasures.[12] In the case of the lecherous, the author cited Exodus 34: 20: 'but the firstling of an ass thou shalt redeem with a lamb'. Here, the bestiary author implied that the firstborn of the ass, an unclean animal and symbolic of the worldly, represented the beginning of a life of lechery unless remitted to Christ. The lamb, emblematic of Christ's sacrifice for humanity and its sins, symbolised purity and innocence.[13] As for the lustful and wanton, the author recalled Ezekiel 23: 20: 'for she (the Israelites) doted upon her paramours, whose flesh is like the flesh of asses' – comparing the perceived intense lust of the ass with that of the sinful and idolatrous Israelites.

Spiritually, Bodley 764 also presented the ass's brutish and lecherous nature ('brutum et libidinorum') as characteristic of the pagan people ('gentilem populum . . . significat') over whom Christ was a worthy ruler and leader towards salvation ('ad celestem patriam per duceret').[14] The image of Christ riding an ass went beyond that of a ruler riding a humble ass; in this case, the ass that Christ rode into Jerusalem represented the pagan people subjecting themselves to Christ's authority. That the bestiary was written from a Christian perspective should also alert us to its implicit meanings embedded in the examples. By using a series of Old Testament examples, the Bodley 764 author censured Jews without explicitly stating their name, yet they provided the lecherous, wanton and foolish examples. Whilst ultimately the ridden ass mirrored the yoked Christian – each a faithful servant – the examples reminded medieval readers that not only were the Jewish people yet to submit to Christ's authority, but that God was the ultimate judge.[15]

Other bestiary authors were less cautious in their judgemental writings against the Jewish peoples. The Anglo-Norman poet Philippe de Thaon wrote the earliest versified and vernacular bestiary (1120s), for Henry I of England's first wife, Adeliza.[16] In the preface, he unequivocally denigrated the Jews, comparing them to the ass:

> E par l'asne entendum
> Judeu par grant raisun.
> Asne est fols par nature,
> Si cum dit Escripture;
> Ja n'istrat de sa rute
> Se l'em ne li tolt tute.
> Tut itel nature unt
> Li Judeu ki fol sunt;
> Ja en Dé ne crerunt
> Se par force nel funt;
> Ja n'ierent cunverti
> Se Deus n'en ait merci.

> By the ass we understand
> The Jews by great reason.
> The ass is foolish by nature,
> As the Scripture says;
> Never will he depart from his way
> If one does not drag him entirely from it.
> Just such nature have
> The Jews who are fools;
> Never in God will they believe
> Unless they do it by force;
> Never will they be converted
> Unless God has mercy on them.[17]

It is evident that Philippe used the ass's perceived foolish and stubborn behaviours to depict the Jews, two medieval stereotypes that were commonly ascribed to the Jews.[18] This section was not a beast entry per se, but formed part of the introduction and dedication to the queen.

In this didactic text, Philippe introduced the supremacy of the lion as a metaphor for Jesus and Christianity whilst reminding the queen of Jewish perfidy. He invoked the common medieval perception that Christ died at the hands of the Jews and that He will have vengeance via the lion's claws, '[p]ar les ungles entent des Judeus vengement' ('by the claws, is meant vengeance upon the Jews', line 38). In another example of the Jews' defiance, Philippe specified that the angry lion would eat indiscriminately, including asses who resist and bray (lines 41–4). Why Philippe chose to depict the Jews in such a discriminatory manner by likening them to asses has not yet received scholarly attention. Considering that most bestiaries, including this one, mirrored the *Physiologus*, this bestiary stands out for its edifying dedication. By the 1120s, when Philippe wrote his bestiary, England had its second or third generation of Jews, having been originally invited by William the Conqueror (1066–89) to stimulate English commerce and the economy. Jews had royal protection and privileges, but Jewish pogroms on the Continent, especially during the First Crusade (1095–9), would have been well-known across Europe by this time. Either Philippe was merely repeating commonplace sentiments towards the Jews – there were increasingly aggressive and violent attitudes on the part of Christians to cement their religion as the pre-eminent faith – or he was using his bestiary to impose his own religious prejudices on Henry's new queen.[19] Regardless, and perhaps ironically, he found in the ass a flexible and willing beast to emphasise the medieval Christian-held pejorative view of the Jews as a stubborn and foolish people.

Christ riding an ass into Jerusalem marks a critical point in the history of the Jewish and Christian faiths – the rupture from Judaism to Christianity. For medieval authors, the holy ass crossed this religious breach with ease. The bestiary ass, adversely represented as stubborn and foolish or devilishly braying incessantly, could either be representative of the Jews and their faith or symbolic of a hungry devil seeking nourishment. In every case, bestiary readers recognised that humility and faithfulness were the ways to salvation.

THE SAINTLY ASS

Christ may have been the ultimate holy figure associated with the ass, but saints also held an exalted position in the heavenly hierarchy, often through their relationship with animals. St Francis of Assisi, known for his love of animals, preached to birds, blessed a variety of animals and, according to his biographer, Saint Bonaventure, brought a live ass into the Christmas Mass to stand with an ox over a manger.[20] Francis even referred to his body as *frater asinus* ('brother ass') in reference to the bodily scourging that an ass endured, and that Francis inflicted on himself to subdue his sensual nature.[21] Bellini's fifteenth-century painting *St Francis in the Desert* (*c.* 1480) has been argued by art critics to illustrate the moment of Francis's stigmata.[22] He is depicted alone in his cell amidst a metaphorical wilderness. The city in the background is further removed from Francis via the desolate field in which stands a solitary onager, the wild ass of the desert, and a symbol for monks who shunned the secular world. Although Francis became a mendicant rather than a regular monk, Bellini's ass symbolised Francis as a hermit, seeking solitude in his quest to serve God.

Just as Bellini's depiction of Francis with an onager is an artistic construct, hagiographers also fashioned stories about saints and their special relationships with animals, which included the ass. An early Egyptian Desert Father, Abbot Helenus, was aided on an arduous journey by a herd of wild asses. When he called on them to help him, invoking Christ in his plea, they spontaneously heeded his call and carried him and his load for the rest of the journey.[23] St Jerome exhibited a similar authority over beasts. In his legend of a lion and an ass, although it is the lion's obedience and submission that is central to the myth, the king of the beasts must take on the ass's burdensome duties after failing to keep the ass secure.[24] Jerome's and Helenus's hagiographers demonstrated the saints' divine power through the willing compliance of wild animals. The two saints' control over the untamed beasts pointed to their exalted state and evoked the prelapsarian state in Eden, when Adam had dominion over the animals.

Equally exceptional are the deeds of Sainte Foy (Foi or Faith) of Conques. Recorded in her 'Book of Miracles' are five miracles attributed to the saint that concern the ass and unnatural ass – mule.[25] Four of the five miracles involved the saint effecting the resurrection of a dead ass. In each case the saint did not respond to the ass owners' pleas for help until the ass had died and was about to be flayed. At this point, Sainte Foy intervened and brought the ass back to life. Each ass then bore its skinning wounds as a permanent reminder of the saint's power. Raising animals from the dead was an uncommon miracle, yet Sainte Foy was credited with four, attesting to her divine status and her efficacy as a provider of miracles and as an intercessor.[26]

The resurrection motif served as a lesson regarding redemption and new life within the Christian way of life.

As well as resurrecting asses, Sainte Foy also provided an ass to help a prisoner escape from his captors. The miracle recalled a prisoner held in chains in a tower who prayed to Sainte Foy to help him escape. Not only did she encourage him to leap from the window, bestowing on him the ability to 'float' to earth, she also supplied a celestial ass that carried him to safety before disappearing without trace. The newly liberated prisoner then gave thanks to the saint.[27] Sainte Foy's intercessory powers in this miracle tale invoke the image of the ass and its close association with Christ. Just as the ass carried the Christ Child to safety in a time of danger, Sainte Foy's ass performed a similar salvific task.

Saints' hagiographies and tales of their miracles also served as material for sermons and preaching: to promote the fame and efficacy of saints, attract pilgrims to saints' shrines and promote and justify the Christian message. One of the reasons Bernard of Angers recorded Sainte Foy's miracles was so that the stories could be used in sermons as examples of God's mercy and the powers of saints to reassure faithful and steadfast Christians. As intercessors between God and Christians, saints were the conduit between the heavenly and earthly worlds beseeching God's mercy on a petitioner's behalf. Corresponding to their exceptional position, saints' relationships with animals went beyond the ways in which ordinary Christians interacted with animals. Animals validated a saint's divine power: they voluntarily aided saints, wild animals obeyed saints and helped saints perform miracles, or they became the object of a saint's miracle.

THE FESTIVAL ASS

That animals enacted miracles were not their only perform-ative quality. Real and life-sized imitation asses partici-pated in and vivified Christian ritual and liturgy. St Francis placed a live ass in the nativity stable, and to observe the feast day of Palm Sunday, many medieval towns paraded wooden life-sized asses bearing effigies of Christ through the streets. This practice was especially prevalent within the Holy Roman Empire, where the statue was referred to as Palmesel (literally 'Palm ass').[28] Commemorating Christ's triumphal entry into Jerusalem, the Christological ritual was a solemn occasion and one that Christians could witness and participate in. The laity lined the route of the Palmesel – usually from one church to another – and bowed and waved blessed palm fronds as the three-dimensional Christ-of-the-Entry processed. The ass was a central feature of the liturgical procession, echoing the gospels that said Christ specifically demanded an ass as His steed, and medieval church officials were concerned to maintain biblical integ-rity and propriety. Processional asses that sustained dam-age had to be repaired to high standards or else be forfeited. In one Swabian village, church officials asked a craftsman to continue working on the ass to improve its aesthetic appeal, and at Constance, church officials were alarmed by the poor state of repairs to their Palmesel. The ass was integral to Christ's story, and on Palm Sunday it reminded Christians of its role as the bearer of salvation; on this of all days in the Christian calendar, the ass was an object of dignity.

Another Christian feast day, the *Festum stultorum* ('Feast of Fools'), also sanctified the ass. Taking place in the weeks following the Nativity, and also known as the Feast of the Subdeacons, it was one of four feast days to honour members of the clergy.[30] As with the Easter Palmesel ritual, this rite also had a performative element, but despite being more pronounced and pageant-like than a regular mass, it also remained a solemn occasion that involved a live ass.[31] During the ritual the choir would sing the processional chant *Orientis partibus* whilst an ass was paraded in the church. At the same time, the subdeacons prepared to read from Isaiah (9: 6–7) that foretold one of the messianic prophecies: the arrival of a young king to reign on David's throne forever.[32]

Scrutiny of the composite elements of the Feast of Fools reveals a metaphorical relationship between the ass and the subdeacon, who were respectively literal and figurative beasts of burden serving Christ.[33] Just as the ass carried Christ at key moments in His life, the subdeacon's role was to carry the wine and host – the sacramental Christ – during the Eucharist. The processional chant *Orientis partibus* elevated the status of the ass as it lauded the beast's virtues: strength, hauling and threshing. Eschewing the ass's traditional negative implication of fool, the fool here represented a biblical tradition that signalled the paradoxical relationship between God and Christians. A fool could be either one who denied God and His author- ity, or a foolish, lowly, unworldly Christian. The Feast of Fools honoured the latter via the subdeacons – the lowest members of the clerical hierarchy – and the lowly ass.[34] In using an ass to recognise the value of the subdeacons, the congregation had the opportunity to reflect on Christ's salvatory purpose: the ass carried Christ just as the sub- deacon carried the Eucharist. Like the festivals for Palm Sunday, the Feast of Fools was a solemn occasion.

EMOTIONAL RESPONSES TO THE ASS

Each of the four religious ass-types featured in this chapter – biblical, bestiary, hagiographical, festival – share a common goal: to elicit an emotional response from their audience within a Christian paradigm. Emotions function to concentrate attention and motivate, effecting a behavioural response. In the Middle Ages, emotions were referred to as *passiones* ('passions' or 'sufferings') and *affectiones* ('feelings' or 'affections') whilst *motus* ('motion') denoted movement, especially movement of the soul.[35] The bestiary ass that reminded Christians of their earthly, lecherous behaviours could raise the irascible *passio* shame and stir the soul, such that the reader was moved to more modest behaviours. Sermon stories that told of Sainte Foy's revived ass reminded Christians of Christ's promise of resurrection; the fear of death, ever present on pilgrim routes, could be alleviated by undertaking charitable deeds, praying to Sainte Foy and leaving gifts at her shrine.[36]

One emergent theory from work on the emotions concerns the medieval practice of affective piety.[37] Defined as a form of highly emotional devotion to Christ's humanity, affective piety emphasised His earthly beginnings and end. Although the focus was on Christ, that the ass had a constant presence in these rituals meant that it could play a role invoking *passiones* such as love, joy and sorrow, and move the soul to feel compassion. Reading, hearing or looking at scenes from Christ's life enabled Christians not only to visualise the biblical scenes, but even to imagine themselves present and experience a range of feelings. The thirteenth-century ecclesiastic Richard de Fournival declared that when people saw the actions of past individuals in plays it was as though they were present in the past moment.[38] The ass's presence at critical moments in Christ's life meant that it, too, as a creature and symbol, provided a focus to stir emotions and affective piety towards Christ.

However, performative rituals were even more potent in effecting an emotional response. Rather than the audience hearing about, witnessing or imagining themselves in a scene from Christ's life, the Palmesel enabled them to actively participate. Waving palm fronds and watching Christ process on His ass to the gates of Jerusalem (usually the entry to the Church), medieval Christians became Jerusalemites from AD 33 witnessing the Messiah's arrival on an ass. Although the occasion was an immediate cause for joy, realised in the gospels – the people joyously shouted 'Hosanna' (Matthew 21: 15) – medieval Christians also knew that the ass was bringing Christ to His sacrificial death. In this moment, the *passio* joy moved to sorrow, then love. Christ's humility, embodied in His choice of an ass as a mount and self-sacrifice, revealed His love for humankind and love was a guiding motivation for Christian morality.[39] The ass could also effect an emotional response in medieval Christians through a form of collective integration whereby an emotional relationship developed between participants.[40] Also readily exemplified in the Palmesel, the active participation of a frond-waving Christian could lead to an 'emotional contagion' whereby emotional responses to the event were witnessed, shared and modified. Each participant's response was modified by other participant responses, and individual reactions might change the degree of awareness and emotional responses in others.[41]

At pivotal moments in the Christian calendar, the ass played a leading role in the story of Christ. It could inspire a range of emotions – love, affection, awe, humility – and move Christians to engage with their faith through an emotional attachment to the divine. Religious literature, such as the Bible, liturgies, exegeses and hagiographies, prescribed certain emotions and behaviours; emotional responses made the ass a powerful prop that enabled medieval Christians to engage with the divine.

CONCLUSION

The Bible, bestiary, hagiographical and festival asses high-lighted various ways in which the lowly beast of burden functioned within a Christian paradigm. Through the ass's close association with Christ, it attracted a sympathetic characterisation and provided the ass with its paradoxical reputation in relation to its socio-economic role as a beast of burden. For medieval Christians, Jesus and the ass were similarly holy, humble and exemplary. However, on occasions the ass's exemplary reputation was not always upheld, and this was manifest in the sources that dealt with sinners and non-believers, when the ass reverted to its perceived behaviour as stubborn and foolish.

THE
SCHOLASTIC
ASS

Omne animal est asinus.
Tu es animal.
Ergo tu es asinus.

(Every animal is an ass.
You are an animal.
Therefore, you are an ass.)

(William Heytesbury (*c*.1313–72))

THE OPENING EPIGRAPH, from William Heytesbury's *Sophismata asinina*, situates the ass front and centre in one of the pivotal medieval philosophical debates (what separates human from animal) and two of the chief methods of reasoning (syllogisms and sophisms). To interrogate the theoretical world of the ass, the focus of this chapter moves from the natural and religious worlds into the scholastic realm of medieval cathedral schools and the early universities.

Prior to the turn of the twelfth century most education took place in monasteries and was restricted to those who were preparing to take, or had taken, monastic vows. Oblates and monks read the Bible and writings of the early Church Fathers contemplatively: to know themselves and to know God. By the twelfth century, a new form of educational institution had emerged to meet the changing needs of the secular world: the cathedral school.[1] By the turn of the thirteenth century, the cathedral school was being overtaken by the establishment of universities. Often referred to as the renaissance of the twelfth century, this period ushered in new ways of learning.[2] Education now trained clerics for positions of administration (papal and royal), and rather than taking place within the closed world of monasteries, education occurred in urban centres. Here the seven liberal arts of the *trivium* (grammar, logic, rhetoric) and *quadrivium* (arithmetic, geometry, music and astronomy) flourished. This type of education focused on interrogation via questions (*quaestio*) and debate (*disputatio*) and became known as the scholastic method.[3] Students and masters studied newly translated copies of works by classical authors, especially Aristotle, and in this learned environment, philosophy as a discipline flourished and reason became central to intellectual thought in western medieval Europe.

In this new educational environment, masters and students associated with the ass in philosophical and edifying ways that reflected the ass's stereotypical natural world attributes. The scholastic realm and the beastly ass may seem unlikely stablemates, yet the ass's natural world pejorative overtones of senseless and stupid came to the fore. Whilst asinine students attracted negative attributes that were comparable to those applied to the ass – dullard, dunce, fool – even masters were not exempt from similar censure, inviting criticism for foolishly teaching 'unteachable' students. In the intellectual realm, scholastics often used the ass as an exemplar in debates on reason and rationality. Characterised as an irrational animal, the ass proved a useful foil to demonstrate philosophical arguments on logic and reason, including what it meant to be human as opposed to animal, classifying universals and particulars, the theory of free will, and sophisms.

HUMAN AND ANIMAL: UNIVERSALS AND PARTICULARS

The question of whether humans were separate from the animal world was one that had attracted contemplation, debate and argument long before medieval thinkers tackled it. In the ancient world, philosophers' responses fell roughly into two schools of thought: Neoplatonist and Peripatetics (Aristotelians). The former argued for little to no distinction between animals and humans, even judging animals to be rational, arguing that the degree of rationality defined the two groups. The latter separated humans from the animal world for reasons that included human ability to speak and rationalise.[4] In the early medieval period, the Church Fathers favoured a peripatetic justification: it was humans' capacity for reasoning that separated them from animals and made man superior to the beasts. Augustine exemplified this in his exegesis on the book of Genesis, stating: 'The pre-eminence of man consists in this, that God made him to His own image by giving him an intellect by which he surpasses the beasts.'[5] By the later Middle Ages, however, the boundaries between animal and human were less concrete. Aquinas (1225–74), in his *Summa Theologica*, clearly considered humans part of the animal realm, referring to 'man . . . of all animals', yet he elevated humans to a pre-eminent position within the animal world due to human rationality, writing: 'man excels all animals by his reason and intelligence'.[6] This emerging uncertainty over the animal–human divide was exemplified in the metaphorical deployment of the ass in debates on universals and particulars.

The question of universals was one of the foremost debates in medieval philosophical circles. Essentially a debate about the nature (location) of reality, at its most basic level this was a categorisation system with two leading schools of thought: Realist (for things) and Nominalist (for words).[7] The Realist school held that the commonality of all humans was the reality of humans, as their general similarities terminated in their being. Nominalists located reality in the matter of a particular thing: a human was thus a conceptual term with no reality instantiated in matter. In this way, generalities terminated in the word and not matter – general terms could only ever be nominal, not real, hence nominalism.[8] Put simply, a realist considered the identical colour of two identical objects to be a single colour – a universal (thing) – whereas a nominalist would argue for two distinct colours for two distinct objects, that is, this blackness of one thing and that blackness of the other thing – two particulars (words).[9] The twelfth-century intellectual and logician Peter Abelard (1079–1142) took the middle ground to refute the prevailing arguments. In explaining that the realism case was flawed, Abelard referenced the ass. Using a reductive line of reasoning (*reductio ad absurdum* – 'reduction to absurdity'), Abelard cited Socrates, an ass named Brunellus, and the concepts of the rational and the irrational, arguing that rationality and irrationality could be found in the same thing (individual, genus, species):

Rationality and irrationality are, indeed, in the same individual because they are in Socrates. They are simultaneously in Socrates and Brunellus. But Socrates and Brunellus are Socrates. Socrates and Brunellus are indeed Socrates, because Socrates is Socrates and Brunellus, and this because Socrates is Socrates and Socrates is Brunellus.[10]

He continues, explaining his argument against the Realist understanding of universals and particulars, that:

according to this opinion, Socrates is Brunellus: Whatever is in Socrates other than the forms of Socrates is that which is in Brunellus other than the forms of Brunellus. But whatever is in Brunellus other than the forms of Brunellus is Brunellus. Whatever, then, is in Socrates other than the forms of Socrates is Brunellus. But if this is the case, since Socrates is that which is other than the forms of Socrates, then Socrates himself is Brunellus.[11]

Expressing early nominalist thought, Abelard was able to get purchase for Socrates and Brunellus because of a weakness in the realist argument.[12] If the reality of a thing lay in the commonality of the general form, then Abelard reduced Socrates and Brunellus to the same universal genus – animal. As both Socrates and Brunellus are animals, then that is their reality. Socrates was a rational and irrational man, man is part of the animal genus, the animal genus contains rational and irrational creatures, thus Socrates must be the same as Brunellus – an ass.[13]

Regardless of the seemingly absurdity (or even circularity) of this proposition, the point of interest for this book is Abelard's choice of ass as the defining animal. Abelard was able to draw on the nature of the ass to highlight the irrationality that he then applied to the philosophical debates. The ass was irrational and so was the realist argument on universals.[14] Even in substituting the word 'ass' for Brunellus, Abelard had declared his position on the realist argument: Brunellus, the brown and dull ass, was by association unintelligent. Never one to mince his words, whilst it was absurd to call Socrates an ass, that was Abelard's point; forthright and plainspoken, he used the ass above all other animals to demonstrate his opponents' asinine arguments.

THE INDIFFERENT ASS

Animal behaviour was instinctive – a response to their sensory powers – and it was their lack of intellect that prevented them from making rational decisions.[15] As an animal with a reputation as a senseless beast, the ass was a logical choice for rational humans to highlight the illogical and irrational animal; indeed, Thomas of Cantimpré declared the ass to be 'irrationabile ultra omnia animantia' ('more irrational than all other living creatures').[16] Medieval scholastics applied the irrational ass trope to the theory of free will (or action theory) in their quest to answer two main questions: was will free or determined, and what motivated action – reason or passion (brute desire)? Both can be related to the ass, who clearly comes out on the side of the unfree and brute desire.

The theory of free will had its origins in the writings of the ancient philosophers and started as a theory of indifference – put simply, how did two equal choices influence preference or movement? Starting as a mechanical concept to explain the relationship between the heavens and earth, ancient philosophers, including Socrates, declared that celestial objects if equidistant would remain secure and immovable.[17] Aristotle then introduced a psychological perspective, swapping celestial bodies for the earthly human body.[18] He exemplified the concept of indifference, that negated motive for choice, through the case of a hungry man equidistant from two food choices. Later philosophers further nuanced the concept, introducing personal convenience or the order in which choices appeared to break the inertia of indifference.[19] It was at this point that the problem of indifference became a philosophical problem of choice and the concept of will was introduced.

Like Aristotle, medieval philosophers also used people and food to highlight the matter of indifference, and tended to follow either an intellectualist or a voluntarist line of reasoning. Intellectualists, including the Dominican Aquinas, argued that a person would always select one of two equal options as human intellect allowed for a preference or point of superiority. Human will was capable of cancelling the non-preferential paradox and its subsequent inaction.[20] The voluntarist reasoning was largely promoted by Franciscans, including Peter John Olivi (1248–98), Duns Scotus (1265–1308) and William of Ockham (c.1282–c.1348). They argued that free will provided liberty from indifference and enabled humans to override inertia. Around this time, another scholastic and philosopher, Jean Buridan (c.1295–1358), stepped into the debate. Neither intellectualist nor voluntarist, like Abelard before him, Buridan held the middle ground. He posited that free will had the power to suspend or defer choice, so long as it did not go against reason; for his exemplar he used choice of travel routes to one destination.[21] At this point, you might be thinking 'Wait a minute . . . travel routes? What about Buridan's Ass? Didn't he theorise about free will using an ass exemplar?' The short answer is no – at least, the ass example does not appear in his extant writings. Although the paradox of the inert ass carries Buridan's name – an ass placed equidistant between two equal food choices (hay bales) will be incapable of selecting either and consequently, through its inertia, will starve to death – Buridan was not the author of the paradox. So, considering that there is no evidence that any of the philosophers used an ass as the exemplar to highlight their theories on indifference, how then does the ass come to be associated with this philosophical paradox, and what is its significance?

Ockham was seemingly the first to use the ass in his defence of the liberty of indifference, writing:

> the [human] will is freely available to will something and not to will it . . . To deny every agent this capability for both alternatives alike is to destroy all praise and blame, all counsel and deliberation, . . . and all freedom of the will. And then a man will be no more free by his will than an ass by its sensory appetite.[22]

For Ockham, clearly if a person was determined by nature to act only in reaction, then humans were not free, like the unfree ass motivated by brute desire. Despite Ockham adding to his statement 'as will be shown another time', his extant writings offer no further commentary on the ass and free will.[23] One possible explanation is that he used the ass example not only in defence of his voluntarist understanding of free will, but also in direct disputation with Buridan's theory on indifference during a university debate. Debates such as the *quodlibetal* – an 'ask me anything' format – were high-profile, public and well-attended events. Without prior knowledge of the questions that would be levelled from a range of people, including their opponents, university masters had to respond quickly and confidently to hold the upper ground. Ockham participated in such debates; to one of his recorded *quodlibetal* questions that asked for his opinion on perfect acts and perfect objects, Ockham replied, 'an angel is more perfect than a human being, and a human being is more perfect than an ass', thus accepting a hierarchy of natural excellence rising from animal via human to celestial worlds.[24] Ockham's *quodlibetal* reference to the ass highlights the animal–human divide and hints at the ass as a common exemplar. In contrasting human free will with the ass's sensory appetite Ockham appears to have been defending his voluntarist stance on free will, possibly against Buridan's middle-ground approach during a debate.[25] Although contemporaries, Ockham and Buridan were known to have had differences of opinion on scholastic issues, and each was in France during the 1320s. In either case, it is difficult to see how the reference to the ass was anything but a deliberate, calculated and cutting remark designed to denigrate Ockham's opponents and their theories on indifference.

Ockham's use of the ass to illustrate his argument highlights medieval philosophical perceptions of the beast as a senseless animal devoid of rational thought or free will, reacting instinctively to its sensory appetite. Despite being a theologian, Ockham eschewed the ass's holy reputation, preferring to use only its natural world attributes, and negative ones at that. He omitted any reference to the hard-working ass, focusing solely on the senseless beast as irrational. Thus Ockham appeared to typecast doubters of his theoretical stance on indifference, using the irresolute ass as a symbol of stupidity. In denouncing his opponents, he unambiguously drew on the common perceptions of the ass's nature – senseless and stubborn. If indeed Ockham did make his ass reference in a *quodlibetal* situation, then it must surely be understood as a powerful and public statement of censure against his rival theorists. Buridan's middle ground on the theory of indifference was clearly untenable to Ockham and likening his opponents to a senseless beast, implicated Buridan in Ockham's contemptuous statement. Buridan's ass, a metaphor of inertia, although non-verifiable, probably came out of the medieval university tradition of *quodlibetal* debates.

THE *SOPHISMATA* ASS – YOU ARE AN ASS

Other ass references in medieval philosophical works might also help to explain why Ockham chose an ass to highlight his disregard for alternative indifference theories, and why Buridan came to be associated with a paradoxical ass. Logical enquiry through sophism (*sophisma*) – a carefully assembled, but doubtful or even false sentence or syllogism – was another philosophical consideration that attracted ass allusions. Buridan was one of several early fourteenth-century philosophers to address the complex matter of the *sophisma*. His contemporary sophists included Walter Burleigh (*De Puritate artis logicae tractatus*), Richard Billingham (*Speculum puerorum*) and William Heytesbury (*Sophismata asinina*): all cited the ass. Buridan's *Sophismata* was a work on logic designed to assist his students in cutting through any ambiguity and determining the veracity of a problematic sentence or *sophisma*. Throughout *Sophismata*, Buridan used ass examples to affirm or refute a statement. When Buridan stated the sophism 'I say that man is an ass', he offered an exposition in dialectical tradition that simultaneously confirmed and denied the statement. According to Buridan, it was true because he *said* the statement, but false because man was not an ass. The logician's approach, which determined the veracity of the sophism, drew heavily on a semantical and grammatical analysis of the sentence – Latin word order, subject, predicate, proposition – whilst the sophism's falsity relied on reason (intellect). That *sophismata*, or constructed sentences, usually had a bizarre extraordinary aspect to them served as a student learning tool, making them more memorable.[26] If a sophism at its barest level was understood as a semantic paradox, then who better than the paradoxical and irrational ass to enliven the logicians' word-play exercise?

Regardless of the philosophical outcomes, the point to take from this is the consistent use of the ass. The inductive reasoning in many cases called on the questions of human and animal as belonging to the one genus: if a human was an animal and the ass was an animal, then the reduction to absurdity (*reductio ad absurdum*) technique declared humans to be asses. The indecisive ass in the philosophical issue of free will, unable to choose between two equidistant bales of hay, mirrored the *sophismatic* ass. Each faced a problem of opposing outcomes: equal/unequal true/false. Unable to discern the truth or rational outcome, philosophers manipulated the ass's natural attributes as an irrational, stolid beast to confirm or refute their arguments. If scholastics could pointedly call each other an ass, then there is little reason to doubt their ability or willingness to confer the same status on their students.

STUDENTS AND MASTERS: DON'T BE AN ASS
There is no doubt that some medieval students excelled in their studies – the student Abelard out-argued his master – but others were more academically challenged, and they attracted censure from learned quarters. Whilst university masters invoked the ass to debate complex philosophical questions, some of their students were being compared to asses for their lack of academic aptitude. One image above all others stands testament to this sentiment – the ass and lyre (or harp) (Illustration 4).

There is ongoing debate surrounding the origins of this image and how it should be understood in its medieval context, it stemmed from either Boethius's sixth-century *De consolatione philosophiae* ('The Consolation of Philosophy') or the Greek fabler Phaedrus and his fable *Asinus ad lyram* ('The Ass and the Lyre').[27] Boethius's famous quote in which the Lady Philosophy asks the author, have her words penetrated his mind or is he as 'dull as the ass to the sound of the lyre?' and 'Can you grasp this, or does such knowledge transcend your understanding? 'highlights a mental process whereby comprehension and understanding were not abilities of which everyone could avail themselves.[28] Conversely, Phaedrus's

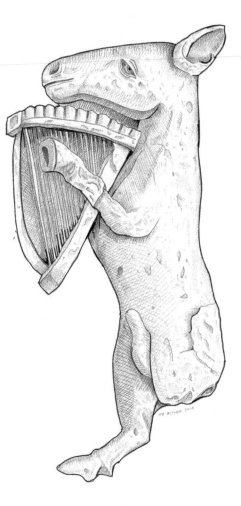

Illustration 4: *Ass Playing a Lyre*, based on the south portal at the church of Saint Pierre, Aulnay de Saintonge, France. Illustration by Mr Alford.

fable features an ass who, on finding a lyre, discovers that he cannot mirror human capabilities and make melodious music – hooves being no substitute for dextrous hands. The accompanying moral cautioned against those who challenged their inherent nature.

The main difference between the two examples, and how they should then be applied and understood, hinged on passive listening or active playing. The Boethian passive listener was most likely exemplified in medieval church sculptures of lyre-playing asses. Here, the imagery signified the illiterate unlearned who believed in, but could not articulate, the divinely revealed Christian truths. An ignorant but faithful Christian was not to be reproached for an inability to understand matters of faith at a higher level. These were Christians that Peter Lombard (c.1096–1160) termed 'simple' in his seminal work, *Sentences*. Invoking Job (1: 14), 'The oxen were ploughing and the asses feeding beside them', Lombard equated the simple Christian with the she-ass, whilst the oxen alongside represented the learned elders offering guidance.[29] In twelfth-century intellectual circles, the oxen became representative of preachers whose task was to instruct the simple, or the she-ass: 'Boves sunt . . . prelati . . . Asine dicuntur simplices . . . Est ergo sensus, quod prelate debent instruere simplices' ('Oxen are . . . prelates . . . Ass is called simple . . . So the meaning is, that the prelate ought to instruct the simple').[30] Reflecting a Boethian awareness, simple Christians might not be able to explain articles of faith, but thanks to their elders, they implicitly believed nonetheless. The ass–lyre church sculptures served to remind all Christians that, regardless of intellect, the faithful were welcome in God's house. Indeed, the south portal location of the sculpture of the lyre-playing ass (Illustration 4) would serve as a constant reminder to the congregation of the simple but faithful and thus worthy Christian, every time they entered through that door. Yet a Boethian ass, however sympathetic its interpretation, was still less than the ideal of human behaviours. In medieval society status was partly intellectually derived and in the natural world order the unlettered, like asses, were not intellectually equipped to consider the divine.

The active player applied more to the academic environment of education concerning student and master. Just as Phaedrus's fable cautioned, people who tried to rise above their natural, inherent ability, but failed, showed themselves to be like the ass that tried to do something for which it was not equipped. Here, the lyre-playing ass imagery was located in the student environment as a metaphor for the uninformed, rather than the unlettered.[31] Scrutiny of the ass in three historiated initials from twelfth-century manuscripts – Josephus's account of 'The Jewish War', Aristotle's 'Prior Analytics' and an alphabetical list of Hebrew names in Jerome's 'Questions on Genesis' – reveal a didactic relationship between text and image. Drawing on an oppositional relationship between the ass images and texts, the images imply folly whilst the texts affirm wisdom. The ass and its absurd, even pointless, activities signify the futility of some scholars unsuited to learning, as well as some teachers who did not meet their expected scholarly responsibility to educate only the most capable.

In the copy of Josephus's text, the illumination juxtaposes a foolish ass with the author's opening condemnation of alternative, unreliable accounts of the war, thus censuring other authors' inferior works and mediocre teaching. The folly of the lyre-playing ass censured those who taught improperly, lest they proved themselves to be fools. John of Salisbury, another twelfth-century cleric and philosopher, likewise used this form of censure against a false teacher who was 'less clever' than previous teachers and 'thrashed the air for a long time' and 'taught his credulous listeners to know nothing'.[32] The association of ass and unsuitable teacher is also underscored in the copy of Jerome's text 'Questions on Genesis', where the lyre-playing ass informs the definition of 'Aethiopia' as ignorance and darkness. The imagery in the historiated letter 'A' further reveals a didactic message regarding false teachers. A naked man, opposite the lyre-playing ass, wields a whip-like object that was associated with teachers as well as being used in beast management. The man's nakedness alerts the reader to his natural state, unsuited for his apparent occupation, and in conjunction with the text serves as another caution against unsuitable teachers. Such imagery was a concept that any medieval biblical exegete would have been familiar with. The second epistle of Peter had already likened false teachers to irrational animals (2 Peter 2: 12), and the ass had long been recognised as an irrational beast, if not the superlative irrational beast.[33]

In the twelfth-century copy of Aristotle's 'Prior Analytics', the didactic focus moves from the teacher to the student. The illumination of an ass appearing to tune a lyre – an activity to which it is most unsuited – highlights the gaucheness of the ass and serves as a contradiction to the accompanying text concerning ways of demonstrating understanding. Clearly the lyre-tuning ass does not understand its limitations and is yet another visual representation of folly. The same manuscript contains another Aristotelian text, 'Sophistical Refutations'. This also includes ass imagery, as two naked men engage in debate, one with an ass's head and the other holding a banner with the words 'if you are an ass'. Didactically, this image warned against taking things at face value. It also echoes a sentiment voiced by Abelard regarding the education of unworthy students: like asses with lyres, unworthy students are incapable of understanding their textbooks.[34] One other ass that epitomised the sentiment of a foolish student and that would have been well known to medieval audiences was Brunellus, the *Speculum Stultorum*'s ass. This literary ass travelled across Europe and spent seven years as a student at the university in Paris. Eventually he was thrown out, unable to recall any of his studies, such was his innate inability to learn.

The lyre-tuning, debating and fictional student ass imagery epitomised and censured those who tried to learn but failed because of their inherent lack of academic ability. Medieval images of lyre-playing asses provided instructive observations about logic and learning from a student and master perspective, in that they emphasised the value of education and the futility of teaching the stubborn or foolish. The ass informed within a learned environment based on pre-existing perceptions of the beast. A consideration of the ass in its natural world, juxtaposed with the ass-lyre imagery alluded to the natural world in which the inherent order was disrupted as the beast attempted to engage with something it could not understand.

CONCLUSION

In medieval universities and cathedral schools, reason and rationality dominated philosophical debates.[35] The ass, as a symbol of irrationality, contradicted intellect and was a useful counter to emphasise a philosophical debate or theory. It could also censure teachers and students. Relying predominantly on the ass's natural world negative attributes, medieval scholastics used the ass in personal slights that were simultaneously acerbic and humorous – the thought of Socrates masquerading as an ass is at once impudent and disrespectful, yet boldly mischievous. The ass metaphor could disparage or discredit. Invoking the ass reflected stubbornness – scholastic opponents were obdurate and inflexible, holding to asinine theories, whilst the stubborn student was unwilling or unable to learn.

THE ASS IN
LITERATURE

I'm not the wise Brunellus, but a dolt,
An ass forever, prince of fools, a dunce.
A fool I was when born, a fool before,
And nothing but a fool shall always be.

(Nigel Wireker (*c.*1130–*c.*1200), *Speculum Stultorum*)

CONSIDERING THE WAYS in which people knew and interacted with the ass, it is unsurprising to see imaginative expressions of the ass appear in works of fiction – fables, fabliaux, novels, beast epics, poetry. In the fictional world of medieval literature, the many stereotypes of the ass collided to present an ass that was at one time or another senseless, stubborn, hard-working, exemplary, sanctified, sexualised and politicised. This chapter highlights the versatile ass from four viewpoints – didactic, comedic, political, sexual – theorising the literary ass from a gendered perspective.

THE DIDACTIC ASS

There is a scholarly consensus that all medieval literature had a didactic purpose, and the sixth-century BC Aesopian fables are one of the most readily acknowledged medieval didactic genres.[1] Copied, reworked and translated by a range of authors, by the Middle Ages the fables were used as a formal educational text for schoolboys and university students. Preachers incorporated them into their sermons as *exempla*, and fable imagery was recorded in sculpture, manuscript illumination and tapestries. The lessons contained within the fables were moralistic, aimed at teaching socially appropriate behaviours. As exemplars for humans, fable animals had an allotted place in the world and reminded people of their place in the social hierarchy. The ass's natural world attributes often came to the fore in the fables where it epitomised the medieval peasantry: subjugated, uncouth and at the bottom of the social hierarchy.

In the fable 'Of the Lion and the Ass', an ass insulted a lion and the lion resisted taking its revenge. According to the fable, the lion represented the learned, noble and virtuous, whereas the ass was symbolic of the ignorant. Another ass metaphor occurred in the fable 'Of the Ass and the Lapdog'. In this fable, an ass was jealous of its master's dog, who enjoyed the master's affections whilst the ass toiled unrewarded. When the ass tried to emulate the dog by sitting on its master's knee, it earned a beating for almost killing the master. The fable's appended moral, or epimythium, cautioned those who held ambitions beyond their social boundaries. In each of these tales, the senseless and foolish ass represented foolishly ambitious, or asinine, peasants who were censured for daring to transgress their social boundaries.

Many fables then, asserted that one's nature was fixed and inescapable, and the ass was a useful substitute for the subjugated. By the Middle Ages, the Aesopic fables were not the only literary genre to communicate this mindset. The old French fabliaux, described as *contes-à-rire* ('funny stories' or 'tales to laugh at'), were humorous tales, often ribald, that taught lessons on the human condition.[2] The fabliau *Le Vilain asnier* ('The Peasant Ass-driver') underlined the belief that one's place in medieval society was inflexible and immovable, through the presence of two asses. In this tale, an ass-driver carting animal dung through a town took a wrong turn and ended up in the sweet-smelling spice bazaar. Overwhelmed by the pleasantly fragrant scents, he fainted, and only recovered when someone wafted pungent dung beneath his nose. The tale ended with the adage, 'ne se doit nus desnaturer' ('one should not disnature oneself').[3] In this fabliau, the asses not only signposted the protagonist's social status, but they also reinforced and legitimised a social hierarchy: as a peasant, the ass-driver belonged to the earthy world of the peasantry. The fabliau moral clearly taught that nature was inherent and immutable.

A senseless and foolish ass was not the only way that medieval authors used the beast of burden educationally. Marie de France's fables repositioned and reworked the Aesopic tradition to represent the feudal world of twelfth-century Anglo-Norman England. Marie used her fables educationally to inform people about morally correct behaviour. One way she achieved this was through the vice–virtue cycle. She used animals to caution her audience against the vices, particularly the pre-eminent vices of pride and avarice and their associated subcategories – arrogance and bragging, jealousy and ambition. For Marie, the ass became a metaphor for pride and arrogance.

In her reworking of the fable 'The Ass and the Lion', an overconfident ass assumed brotherhood with a lion. Affronted by the ass's arrogance, the lion challenged the ass, who braggingly claimed that the lion did not have the monopoly on ferocity. On top of a hill, the ass brayed loudly to the animals below, who quickly dispersed. The ass then proudly turned toward the lion and boasted of his fearsomeness. The lion retorted that it was the ass's awful cry, not its strength, which made the animals flee; the fable calls to mind the encyclopaedists who wrote about the ass's cacophonous braying. Marie ended with a caution against the arrogant who used threats and quarrelsomeness to frighten people. The ass's pride once more came to the fore in Marie's fable of 'The Boar and the Ass', where an arrogant and proud ass would not yield to a boar. The tale concluded with a caution to the overconfident, who come to harm rather than acquiesce to humility.

The medieval fabliaux and fables can be read as didactic texts that mirrored feudal–aristocratic values and anxieties. They were conservative genres located in their immediate sociocultural context. In a changing world with potential for social mobility and an emergent new social class of merchant and town dweller, fables and fabliaux championed the status quo.[4] They promoted a moral order that justified and maintained the established feudal hierarchy and the needs of the aristocracy. The ass, at times foolish, earthy, self-important and arrogant, was certainly a metaphor for the peasantry, but in Marie's fables the ass also highlighted moral defects, such as pride and arrogance, and emphasised medieval concerns about morality through the vices.[5]

THE COMEDIC ASS

Although the term didactic suggests serious and thoughtful, there is no doubt that many of the fables would have elicited laughter from their audiences, implying that comedy and didacticism were mutually compatible: the audience learns a lesson whilst laughing. The fable ass who wore a lion's pelt to frighten other animals, but brayed rather than roared, conjures a comical image that reinforces the enduring state of inherent nature. When Chaucer's Wife of Bath recounted that King Midas was given the ears of an ass for believing that the god of nature, Pan, was a better musician than the god of music, Apollo, the audience might have laughed at the image of a person with long asinine ears. They understood the tale as a censure against the ignorant who failed to hear and were foolish, like the ass. Comedy was a useful didactic tool.

The fabliaux were arguably the epitome of a medieval comedic genre whose objective was to teach whilst entertaining. Unlike the fables, the fabliaux did not anthropomorphise animals, yet when animals appeared in the fabliaux, they contributed to the comedic outcomes. In the fabliau *Le Testament de l'Asne* ('The Testament of the Ass'), an ass is the antithesis to the human protagonists.[6] This fabliau tells of a money-grabbing, greedy priest who owned an ass. After twenty years of loyal service and hard work the ass died ('li asnes morut de viellesce qui molt aida a la richesse' – 'the ass died of old age who had helped [the priest accrue his] wealth', lines 37–8). The priest was so overwhelmed with sorrow that he had the animal buried in the church cemetery – a place reserved for Christians. When the bishop – overly generous, but drowning in debt – discovered the ass's final resting place, he called the priest to account for his actions. The priest explained that over the ass's loyal years of service the animal had saved its earnings and left it to the bishop in its last will and testament. The bishop accepted the legacy, uttered a blessing for the ass, and the beast remained in consecrated ground.

The fact that the priest expressed grief over the ass's death underscored emotional responses to animal–human interaction. The fabliaux, however, were not known for their tender emotions; rather, in this case, it was the priest's action that led to a raucous emotion – mirth. The image of an ass being interred in a cemetery must surely have triggered some laughter from the audience, thanks to the ridiculousness of the priest's exploit. Dead asses were usually left to rot outside the town or village boundaries, and in the Christian tradition animals were excluded from the afterlife.[7] Any reference, then, to the ass partaking in the hereafter – a human-only exercise – emphasised the comical, and the ass's burial was the catalyst for a series of farcical moments. In justifying the beast's last resting place, the legacy – a cover for a bribe – became the substitute for the burial payment. It was also the means to deliver the ass from hell, as the bishop blessed the ass and asked God to grant the ass salvation and forgive it its earthly faults and sins: 'Hé, dist l'esvesques, Dieus l'ament / et si li pardon ses meffais / et toz les pechiez qu'il at fais' ('Well then, said the bishop, [may] God improve its situation / and pardon its transgression / and all the sins that it has done', lines 158–60).

In this fabliau, comedy and, by implication, its emotional response, laughter, were used to affect a response in the audience.[8] The ass was the foil for the human protagonists, who exemplified greed, pride and avarice (for material possessions rather than a sexual lust). The priest and bishop coveted and longed for material possessions as a show of wealth. The greedy priest was willing to pay any amount of money to get his own way, whilst the bishop would accept any amount of money to secure his financial position. Each mocked the authorised rituals of the Church, highlighting clerical abuses. Meanwhile the hard-working, obedient, faithful ass was not just an exemplar of humility but became the exemplary Christian, epitomised by its Christian burial.

In medieval society, being a virtuous Christian was the only way to achieve eternal life in heaven, and this meant avoiding the virtue's antagonists: the vices. In the 'Testament of the Ass' each cleric was a parody of the avaricious, proud and greedy. The fableor pricked the conscience of the audience: to be a good Christian required loyalty, hard work and obedience. These were all attributes that the ass naturally represented; but for Christians they required more effort, and the priest and the bishop failed to set the good example of model Christians.

Comedy and its consequence – laughter – was (and is) used to censure individuals and groups; it could also define social norms, as well as alleviate social anxieties.[9] In medieval literature, laughter was used as an emotional response to a comic situation to affect certain behaviours. The ass was a versatile comedic tool, serving as an ideal, or less than ideal, model.

THE POLITICAL ASS

The ass was a useful foil to criticise political rivals and those in positions of authority. William of Malmesbury (c.1095–c.1143), John of Salisbury (c.1115/20–80) and Gerald of Wales (c.1146–c.1223) each censured illiterate Norman and Angevin rulers as ignorant, likening them to an *asinus coronatus* ('crowned ass').[10] Although these three erudite authors did not use overt humour to censure (John of Salisbury did employ subtle satire), they still found in the ass's accepted attribute of foolishness a way to express disapproval for illiterate kings who could not understand works produced for them by learned clerics. In this way, the ass was used in the political sphere to reproach the powerful for their ignorance.

Another English king assigned the ignominious title of crowned ass was Richard II (r.1377–1400). His unflattering title, which appeared during the reign of his successor, Henry IV, provided a political justification for Henry's rule – having essentially taken Richard's throne in dubious circumstances. In Richard's case, rather than refer to an illiterate king, the crowned ass indicated an ineffective ruler. During and after Richard's reign, various authors assigned the ass symbolically to Richard. Some drew on the earlier medieval prophecies of the Arthurian wizard, Merlin, that Geoffrey of Monmouth had first incorporated into his 'History of the Kings of England' (*Historia Regum Britanniae*, *c*.1135). Merlinian prophecies offered writers the opportunity to read and rework them as political commentary lauding or vilifying rulers. One such poem, the Anglo-Norman 'The Six Kings to Follow John' (first written around 1312, and then reproduced and reworked in the fifteenth century), announced the fifth king to follow John – Richard II – as an ass. This poem described the ass-king as having feet of lead and the head of an ass, unmistakably a reference to a slow, ignorant, beastly king and clearly a partisan attempt used by Henry IV's supporters to malign Richard.

English authors, however, were not the only ones to pillory Richard. The French poet Eustache Deschamps (1340–1404), in a series of poems about the French–English conflict during the second and third phases of the Hundred Years War (1369–99) likened Richard (and the English) to an ass. Richard was 'l'asne pesant' ('burdensome ass') implying a deficient mental capacity who also had 'pié de plom' ('feet of lead'). In a Merlinesque prophecy, Deschamps also declared that the French king, Charles the Sixth, would 'l'Asne conquerir' ('defeat the ass [Richard]') and regain French lands lost to Edward III.[11] Deschamps used political prophecy as propaganda to encourage Charles to take on the English. In doing so, he drew on the bestiary tradition of the ass as a sluggish, easily subjugated beast as a parallel for Richard: a slow-to-react, foolish and ignorant king whose policies led to the English loss of lands in France.

The ass's natural world attributes were expedient and effective when exploited to denounce political and powerful enemies. The reproach could be caustic without humour; but other political asses did use humour as a tool of reproach. One such political ass was Brunellus, the anti-hero in Nigel Wireker's *Speculum Stultorum* ('Mirror for Fools'). This late twelfth-century tale, set in a monastic realm, tells of an ass who wants a longer tail to match its long ears. It goes on a fruitless journey and after many escapades it ends its journey with the opposite of its desires: a shorter tail as well as shorter ears. This tale was a culmination of literary expression that, through comedy, drew on the fables, nature and vices to produce an ass that provided censure of a political and ecclesiastic nature.

The political situation in which Brunellus found himself is at first glance one of monastic discord, and the *Speculum Stultorum* has generally been understood as a cautionary, satirical tale of monastic abuses, monks being less contemplative and more acquisitive. More recent scholarship on in-house conflict at Canterbury's Christ Church has further nuanced the tale of Brunellus as a personal exhortation to one man to reconsider his candidacy for the position of Archbishop of Canterbury: William of Longchamp, the Bishop of Ely and Richard I's Justiciar of England.[12] Nigel dedicated the tale to William.

Within the epic poem, Nigel relied on a variety of examples to press his point. He was inspired by the fable of *The Ass and the Lion Skin* and applied the fable's moral, that one cannot escape one's allotted nature, to reproach William. Although Nigel conceded that William held powerful positions in secular society, holding the lion's sceptre and kingdom and giving laws to the people, he declared that Brunellus 'semper asellus erit' ('will always be an ass', line 58).[13] William was a political animal who held secular positions of power as chancellor and justiciar of England (1190–1) in the Lionheart's absence on crusade. In these positions he literally held the king's symbols of authority, and in the animal kingdom the ruler was the lion. Yet despite his exalted political positions, Nigel reminded William of his monastic roots – you will always be an ass.

Nigel also cautioned against excessive pride. When Brunellus boasted that he had acquired the necessary potions to make his tail longer – in reality, quack medicine – he quickly lost the concoctions, evoking the popular idiom that pride comes before a fall. Brunellus could never avoid his innate self. When he enrolled in university with the intention of learning, he betrayed his inherent nature as a senseless beast. He was finally kicked out after seven years, having learnt nothing more than how to say 'heehaw', which even he ironically acknowledged he could say prior to becoming a student. Brunellus was impervious to good advice regarding his nature: Galen, the doctor with whom he consulted regarding medicine to procure his longer tail, fruitlessly counselled him to be satisfied with what he had. Ultimately, Brunellus's asinine nature won out and led him back to his master, who subjugated him by cutting his ears to match his short tail.

There is gentle comedy throughout *Speculum Stultorum* that offers a cautionary, satirical tale of monastic abuses. Symbolically, Brunellus as an overly ambitious, proud and foolish ass is representative of an ambitious monk. To understand Brunellus as a political ass means moving beyond the literary world of the *Speculum Stultorum* and locating the tale in its immediate historical contexts. In a religious, secular and political context, *Speculum Stultorum* was a tale that politicised the situation at Canterbury as well as one man's political ambitions. Brunellus was a political ass whose exploits served as a metaphor to caution William of Ely, who was caught up in royal and monastic politics.

Politically, animals were useful metaphors to scorn (and laud) the powerful. Animals with negative reputations offered opportunities for political commentary and criticism. The power of nature translated into a language of power. The natural world attributes of the ass tapped into anxieties concerning times of crises, contests of power, and contempt for the uneducated in positions of power.

THE SEXUAL ASS

In medieval literature, authors also drew on the distinct sexual proclivities of the ass (and ass types) that set it apart from other animals. Authors found inspiration in the natural world ass as a lustful beast that went against nature by mating with other species, and some even imagined that the ass could mate with humans. Inspiration might have come from real-life experiences such as the hybrid mule, whilst others were a misunderstanding of a natural attribute – the spurious association between braying and lust; a few, such as the onocentaur, were purely fantastical. Undeterred, encouraged even, medieval authors sexualised the ass to achieve comedic and didactic outcomes that often re-worked fable, *roman* (novel) and bestiary asses.

In a fourteenth-century Spanish text, 'The Book of Good Love' (*Libro de buen amor*, *c.*1300), Juan Ruiz, a Spanish archpriest, offered lessons through a series of short stories on God's good love and worldly, foolish love that made humans sinful. As a didactic example, he reworked the fable 'The Ass and the Lapdog', exploiting the ass's sexual nature, resulting in a sexualised reading of the fable that was more fabliau-like than fable.[14] In Ruiz's rendition, the dog and the ass shared a mistress rather than master and the attention that the dog lavished on its mistress was highly sexualised. The dog licked and kissed with its tongue and mouth ('con su lengua e boca las manos le besava' – 'with its tongue and mouth licks the hand'), arousing an oral sensualism.[15] The dog also wagged its tail euphemistically before standing on its hind legs to exhibit its masculinity. The location and identity of the dog (small and furry) on its mistress's lap (under a fur wrap) insinuates the sexual nature of the

Illustration 5: 'The Fable of the Ass and Lapdog', in the manuscript La Compilation de Ysopet Avionnet, Bibliothèque nationale de France, BNF Fr. 1594, f.19r.

fable through the lady's relationship with her dog: in medieval beast imagery, small furry animals often symbolised the female sex.[16] When the ass mimicked the dog's actions, it *entered* the mistress's personal space by invading her dais before it *covered* the mistress frontally and placed its forelegs on her shoulders.[17] This action revealed the ass's sexual prowess, as its phallus was exposed and the whole manoeuvre was described in terms more suited to a sexually frenzied stallion ('commo garañón loco el nesçio tal venía' – 'like a mad stud the fool came on').[18] The ass also brayed ('rebuznando'), recalling the sexually frustrated wild asses who brayed to relieve their sexual tensions. As in the original fable, the ass was then severely beaten with phallic-shaped clubs for its transgression.

In a manuscript illumination depicting the traditional ass and lapdog fable (Illustration 5), the artist's positioning of the ass effortlessly evokes Ruiz's retelling of the fable. The ass's upright posture cues a sexual encounter; male asses adopt a semi-upright position during the mating process. The table is set with food – a metaphor for sexual hunger – and the master's servant wields a large shaft-like weapon. Projecting these symbols onto the mistress turned the fable from a moral tale that cautioned against trans-gressing the laws of inherent nature – an ass can never be a lapdog – to a moral tale that cautioned against the dangers of female sexuality. The ass's lusty nature was overlaid onto the lustful woman; just as the ass desired the attention of its mistress and endangered her, so women's desires to possess men sexually were equally dangerous.[19] Ultimately the reworked fable played on the belief that women and asses were lustful creatures and that women succumbed to their animalistic desires.

Another sexualised ass appeared in Boccaccio's plague-inspired *Decameron* (*c*.1350). Dioneo's day five tale (tale ten) detailed a young man, more sexually inclined to men than women, who nonetheless took a wife. As he rarely paid his conjugal debt, his wife became sexually frus-trated and took a clandestine lover. On one occasion, when her husband returned home unexpectedly, the wife hid her lover under the henhouse. A thirsty ass seeking water walked towards the hen coop and stood on the lover's hand, who then yelled out and revealed his presence. Although initially fearful at the consequences of the lover's discovery, the wife provided a monologue about her sexual needs and the husband's disinclination to sexually satisfy her. The husband realised that he must address the situation and executed a plan whereby the lover dined with the couple that evening. Dioneo never stated explicitly what then happened during the rest of the night, but his mischievous remark revealed all:

> But so much as this I know, that on the morrow as he (the lover) wended his way to the piazza, the boy would have been puzzled to say, whether of the twain, the wife or the husband, had had the most of his company during the night.[20]

Boccaccio's positioning of the ass is twofold. First, he projected the image of the ass's unnatural mating habits onto the husband: human male-to-male sex for pleasure, compared with ass-to-horse sex for mule production. Second, Boccaccio exploited a natural impulse – thirst – using it metaphorically for a sexual thirst when he projected the image of a lusty ass onto the lustful wife. Boccaccio revealed his natural world knowledge of the ass and took advantage of the ass's sexual mutability. In doing so, he exploited the ass to reveal a decadent attitude towards pleasure and sexual desire. The result of Dioneo's tale was three sexually satisfied characters, manifesting some of the hedonistic responses to the plague that was ravaging the region.

Boccaccio's thirsty ass had an antecedent in Apuleius's second-century Latin novel *Metamorphoses* (renamed 'The Golden Ass' by Augustine).[21] In this text, the protagonist Lucius was magically, though mistakenly, transformed into an ass rather than a bird. His new ass identity, however, appropriately embodied Lucius's dual human and animal sexual natures. The ass's sexual reputation as a lustful beast was mirrored in Lucius's sexual desires and exploits. That the human Lucius was ass-like pre-empted his transformation into an ass. Lucius's adventures, including his transformation, arose through his curiosity and thirst for knowledge – especially when it pertained to sex. His inquisitiveness about transformation drove him to seduce Photis, the witch Pamphile's servant girl, to learn the secret magic of metamorphosis. During their sexual encounter Photis assumed the dominant position, straddling him, and presaging his impending transformation into a mount. Apuleius also underlined appetite as a metaphor for carnality through the association between food, sex and the ass. Food and drink – their abundance or lack of – featured in many of Lucius's exploits. In an instance where a thirsty Lucius-ass revealed a lover's hiding place by treading on the hiding man's fingers, the adulteress had just prepared a meal for her lover when the husband returned home unexpectedly. Unlike Boccaccio's version of this tale, the result was a sexual encounter between only the lover and cuckold, where the husband 'solus ipse cum puero cubans gratissima corruptarum nuptiarum vindicate perfruebatur' ('lay alone with the boy and enjoyed the most gratifying revenge for his ruined marriage'), before having the boy soundly beaten in the morning.[22]

Apuleius also explored hybrid sex when he had Lucius have sexual intercourse with an unnamed wealthy woman. At this stage in the tale, Lucius had become a sort of circus sideshow, combining his ass body and human mind to perform amazing feats – 'asinum luctantem, asinum saltantem, asinum voces humanas intellegentem sensum nutibus exprimentum' ('a wrestling ass, a dancing ass, an ass who understood what humans said and communicated with sign language').[23] People paid Lucius's owner to see the amazing beast, and one wealthy woman, who made several visits, became infatuated with the ass. She negotiated to spend the night with Lucius, paying handsomely for the experience. Imbibed with alcohol, Lucius overcame his concern that his 'hard hooves' ('duris ungulis'), 'teeth like boulders' ('enormi et gaxeis dentibus deformi') and 'monstrous organ' ('vastum genitale') would injure the woman, and the two engaged in a night of sexual passion.[24] As Lucius described the woman's voracious sexual appetite, it is evident that she led the proceedings, to the extent that Lucius stated that he 'believed that I did not even have enough to fulfil her desire' (deesse mihi aliquid as supplendam eius libidinem crederem').[25] Apuleius's tale of Lucius the ass anticipated not just the medieval conviction that women had a reputation as lustful, sexual beings, but also the ass's repute as a beast that indulged in unnatural sex.

Lucius was a composite beast, much like the fantastical onocentaur recorded in the natural world encyclopaedias and medieval bestiaries. He had a rational and wild side to his character. Physically, unlike the onocentaur, his appearance took on that of an ass in totality; but cerebrally, he could still reason. He had rational human thought but could not speak in human language. He was compelled to live the wordless life of an ass: subjugated and driven by appetite, often of a sexual nature. Lucius's 'libidi sciendi' ('lust for knowledge'), especially of a sexual nature, was grounded in his sensory appetite and is useful for under-standing the ass as a sexual beast.[26] That Lucius desired knowledge and was transformed into an ass is ironic, in the sense that the ass was considered the least knowledgeable of animals, but apposite as the beast associated with lust.

THE GENDERED ASS

Authored by one of few female medieval writers whose work is extant, Marie de France's fables offer an opportunity to examine her work through a gendered lens. She often used animal exemplars in a gendered way that reflected women's position in society. When reworking the *Romulus Nilantii* fables, she identified many of the animals as fem-inine, making implicit statements about power dynamics: male lions represented royalty or nobility, but female sheep stood for the oppressed.[27] Marie might have endorsed the patriarchy of medieval society, but she often used female animal exemplars to instruct and caution against male abuses of power and authority. Thinking about ways in which the medieval ass was gendered raises questions about relationships of power.[28] Medieval cultural entities, such as religion, education and politics, tended to overlook women, or provide limited discussion on their activities and roles beyond the generative and sexualised, allowing male authors to preference men in their writings.[29] The medieval ass became a cultural symbol highlighting the inequalities between men and women, specifically female subjection to male prerogative.

Boccaccio and Apuleius used the ass to denote the woman's subjugated nature. In each instance, whilst women characters tried to exert agency by taking a lover, the ass, the beast known for its subjugation, exposed the wives' infidelity. Their husbands then exercised their authority to remedy the situation to their liking, further subduing the women. For Boccaccio's unfaithful wife, this resulted in a parodic love triangle, emphasising the ludic, unlike Apuleius, whose cuckold's revenge was a display of masculine dominance. In Ruiz's reworking of the ass and lapdog fable, the ass can be understood as a symbol for female lust. It was suppressed by the dominance of the male attendants, signalling men as the controllers of female behaviours. As for Lucius's sexual encounters with the two women, each signalled male authority over women. The amorous woman who eagerly had sex with Lucius was controlled by Lucius's master, as she could only exercise her will if she paid him a fee.

As we have seen throughout this book, the medieval ass was a creature with mutable meanings, and this is also evident when considering the beast from a gendered per-spective. Not only could the ass draw attention to unequal power plays between men and women, it also symbolised power inequities in male relationships, especially within the male-dominated political realm. Likening Richard II to an ass called attention to his weak position as king, within and without his realm. Compared with his political adver-saries, the young king wielded little power and his rule was effectively quelled. In the *Speculum Stultorum*, Brunellus – the foolishly wandering, longer-tail-desiring ass – was a sym-bol for political imbalance. As the personification of the powerful William Longchamp, the ass Brunellus served the author's attempts to curtail William's political ambitions. In an avenue of research yet to be fully explored, the ass's association with unnatural sex may possibly be another reason Nigel Wireker chose an ass as exemplar for William Longchamp. The bishop of Ely had been accused of homosexuality. Hugh of Nonant's open letter accusing William of 'sese feminan simulavit' ('pretending to be feminine') led to his downfall from his exalted secular positions and flight across the English Channel to France and exile.[30] Medieval society considered homosexuality an unnatural sexual practice, and although not performed by Brunellus, the ass was known for its unnatural mating habits. Therefore, the ass could be understood as a symbol for the perverse. That Brunellus had his tail (a symbol of power) docked and that same-sex accusations led to William's exclusion from the English political arena were powerful ways to not only metaphorically emasculate a man, but to manifestly disempower him.

From a gendered perspective, then, the literary ass was a powerful cultural symbol that stressed the differences between men and women as well as occasionally between men and men. Gender legitimised, constructed and reinforced the authority of medieval social institutions, affording male privilege. The gendered ass was representative of the powerless, the weak and the insignificant – usually women; but in the case of William Longchamp, the ass was gendered to bring down a powerful opponent within the male-dominated realms of religion and politics.

CONCLUSION

The literary ass was a capricious beast that transformed and adapted to a variety of scenarios. Medieval authors drew mainly on the ass's natural world, as well as Christian, attributes, to present an ass that was at times senseless, foolish, ignorant, lustful and proud. The literary ass was instructive and humorous. It taught many lessons through metaphor and analogy and offered warnings: socially, members of medieval society were reminded about the inherent and immovable nature of their place in society; religiously, it taught Christian moral lessons on the appropriate behaviours required to attain salvation; it was a political beast that censured powerful opponents; it served as a figure of lust and wantonness; and it highlighted inequalities between men and women that were the result of male-dominated institutions.

POSTSCRIPT
THE MEDIEVAL ASS IN THE POST-MEDIEVAL ERA

The old aunt who was looking after Timothy made rather a fuss and was sure that Ned belonged to someone, but at last she said she would try to find out . . . Ned thought it was very funny. 'As if I ever belonged to anyone,' he said to himself. 'I have always been alone.' But now he wasn't alone any more, for he and Timothy were always together.

(Noel Barr, *Ned the Lonely Donkey: A Story for Children*)

THE RESOLUTION TO the children's story *Ned the Lonely Donkey*, in the epigraph, sees Timothy, a friendless boy, united in companionship with Ned, a solitary donkey; each is no longer alone. Since the ass's domestication, man and beast have been constant companions, with the ass supporting human endeavours. In time, the ass came to be associated with specific attributes. By the end of the Middle Ages (*c.*1500), the ass had a universal reputation as a paradoxical beast. It was remarkable but unremarkable; everyone would have known the ass and, despite its supposed stubbornness, it was outstanding for its work ethic. It was profane and holy; not just the bearer of salvation and an exemplar for the good Christian, it also represented the sinful, the flawed

Illustration 6: *The Journey of a Modern Hero, to the Island of Elba*, originally published by J. Phillips, 32 Charles Street, Hampstead Road, London (1814). Library of Congress Prints and Photographs Division, Washington, DC 20540.

and unbeliever. It was clever but also irrational; Balaam's ass knew not to disobey God's word, whilst proponents of scholastic arguments were reduced to the level of asses – asinine and absurd. It was part of the natural world, although some of its behaviours, and their outcomes (mules), were considered unnatural. The multifaceted impressions of the medieval ass left a legacy that persisted into later historical eras. These final comments highlight a small selection of examples that attest to the enduring heritage of the medieval ass.

THE POST-MEDIEVAL POLITICAL AND IRRATIONAL ASS

Like medieval authors before them, later writers called upon the ass's natural world and literary attributes to censure political enemies. In the sixteenth century, during the turbulent years of the Reformation, religious adversaries produced satirical caricatures that ridiculed their opponents. Lucas Cranach's woodcut of *The Papal Ass* (1523), created to accompany Philip Melanchthon's pamphlet *The Pope-Ass Explained*, presented the pope as a monstrous hybrid, with the head of an ass, a woman's torso, cloven and clawed feet, with a dragon-headed tail, set against a backdrop of Rome.[1] For early Lutherans, the pope was head of a deformed church, and the ass's head symbolised the *caput ecclesiae* ('head of the Church'). Embracing the medieval ass's paradoxical nature, the ass-headed pope represented the inconsistency of papal claims to spiritual authority – as the Roman Church was a spiritual power, how could it have a corporeal head and still claim spiritual authority?[2] For Lutheran polemical authors, the ass-headed pope was stubborn and irrational.

During the nineteenth century, the political ass made several appearances in print media. Towards the end of the Napoleonic Wars (1803–15) when the English exiled Napoleon to Elba, a satirical cartoon appeared in London, titled *The Journey of a Modern Hero, to the Island of Elba* (Illustration 6). In this sketch, Napoleon was depicted riding backwards on an ass, holding the ass's tail in one hand and a broken sword in the other. Text emanating from the ass's rear, seemingly in a stream of flatulence, declared that 'the greatest events in human life is turn'd [*sic*] to a puff', whilst another line of text contrasted Napoleon's throne with the ass's seat – 'a throne is only made of wood and cover'd [*sic*] with velvet' – indicating the modest nature of each seat. Unlike Christ, who rode an ass with majesty, Napoleon rode his ass as a symbol of his excessive pride and broken ambition.

Another nineteenth-century political ass, and one that still endures today, is the American Democratic Party's ass. This figure is emblematic of a medieval contrarian ass: stubborn and steadfast. During Democrat Andrew Jackson's presidential campaign (1828), his opponents called him an ass (jackass) to deride him as 'ornery' and stubborn. However, Jackson embraced the figure of the ass and stressed its steadfast and strong-willed characteristics as qualities to be upheld, rather than ridiculed. When the cartoonist Thomas Nast (1840–1902) later used the ass in his political cartoons, he further popularised the ass as the symbol of the Democrat Party.

Even in our modern world the figure of the political ass remains current. During the uncertainty and commotion of Britain's attempts to negotiate a smooth exit from the European Union – aka Brexit – a grass-roots campaign appeared (2019). The campaign, called 'Led by Donkeys', saw organisers pasting copies of politician's tweets to billboards to remind the public of some of their elected representatives' double standards on Brexit.[3] As well as being political in nature, the billboard campaign had a fable-like nature. The organisers' sentiment that Britain was a 'nation of lions being led by donkeys' suggested that the ass-like politicians had risen above their inherent nature to usurp the lion's position. As the tweets exposed, the politicians' unsuitability to fulfil the roles of Brexit leaders was clear evidence of their asinine nature.

The irrational ass of the medieval scholastic world has also intruded into the political post-medieval world. During the American government's debate to decide the location of the Atlantic–Pacific canal – Panama or Nicaragua – a cartoon (*c.*1900) depicted Congress in a Buridan's ass paradox.[4] The cartoon ass carried the Senate on its flanks like two panniers, whilst the dome of Congress sat atop the ass's head. On either side of the ass were two hay bales, labelled Panama and Nicaragua. The message was that Congress, the apex of the American political organisation, had been reduced to a vacillating, perplexed beast, unable to decide on a location, as each were equally tempting options. Whilst this cartoon was evidently political in nature, it also showed how medieval philosophical debates could be revived in twentieth-century imagery. The cartoonist used humour and a philosophical debate – absence of preference – to reduce the American Congress to asininity.

In the irrational world of the literary ass, Sancho and his steadfast ass in the Spanish novel *Don Quixote* (1605/15)

can be understood as foils, albeit contradictory ones, for the irrationality of Sancho's master, Don Quixote. Rather than the ass representing irrationality, it was Don Quixote who was the foolish character. Quixote, absorbed in a past era of chivalry, assumed the persona of a knight errant and embarked on a journey to rejuvenate the age of chivalry. He constantly misread a variety of situations, and Sancho, his reliable earthy companion, constantly rescued him. Sancho was a metaphor for his ass: at times stubborn, he was treated as a beast of burden, but he was also loyal, faithful and obedient and knew his place in the world – servile and working the land.[5] Sancho and his ass were also Balaam-like. The all-seeing, all-knowing Sancho was contrasted with his metaphorically blind and irrational master. Just as Balaam's ass saved Balaam from God's wrath, so Sancho saved Quixote from a series of mishaps brought about by the master's irrationality and refusal to see the truth in a situation.

THE LANGUAGE OF THE ASS

Medieval society might not have made a sexual association with the ass's name, but medieval authors wrote about the ass's sexual appetite in their encyclopaedia and literary works. Shakespeare recycled this motif when he transformed the character Bottom into an ass (A *Midsummer Night's Dream*, *c.*1600). Bottom was everything an ass was expected to be: stolid and dull. Unlike Apuleius's Lucius (who was the likely inspiration for Bottom), Bottom had no natural sexual curiosity or appetite and was oblivious to Titania's romantic desires. Maybe it was no accident that Shakespeare chose the name Bottom to draw attention to the evident paradox.

Currently, the word ass has taken on more explicit, pejorative meanings; someone might be referred to as an ass, a jackass or a dumb-ass. These terms directly reference the ass's perceived traits as a foolish, unintelligent animal lacking common sense. With the shift in the English vocabulary that now prefers 'donkey' to 'ass', the word ass also has stronger sexual connotations. To get some ass (to have sex) or taking it up the ass (to have anal sex) have entered the vernacular as demeaning slang terms for various types of sexual activity. And of course, who could forget the unforgettable line in Quentin Tarantino's film *Pulp Fiction*, 'I'm gonna git [*sic*] medieval on your ass'. Marsellus Wallace, the character who had just been raped, delivered the much-quoted line as a threat to avenge his vicious violation. Although not directly referencing the medieval ass, Wallace's threat melds two concepts – anal sex, and the medieval world as cruel and debauched.[6]

THE POST-MEDIEVAL WORKING ASS

In the natural world, post-1500 to the present day, the ass has maintained its presence as a beast of burden. In the British Isles, where its medieval presence was limited, it has steadily increased in numbers. Like its medieval ancestor, the ass continued to work in an agricultural environment, although by the nineteenth century its usefulness had extended to a range of non-agricultural and urban environments, especially haulage of merchandise and tools.[7] Today's seaside donkey has its origins in coastal regions as a farm animal.[8] Before the advent of seaside tourism, its original purpose was to transport sand and seaweed to supplement farm pasture: sand to lighten heavy clay soils and seaweed as a fertiliser. As the ass was only required for haulage at certain times of the year, during the summer, with increasing visitors to coastal villages, the ass became a means of holiday transport; at first, probably transporting visitors and their baggage, before being superseded by mechanical vehicles. The seaside donkey, which still provides fun rides for children, is a permanent reminder of its hard-working past.

The ass and hybrid mule have also continued to assist humans in their military endeavours. Their qualities as capable beasts suited to harsh conditions have meant that they have seen active service in a variety of roles and theatres of war: pack work, haulage and riding.[9] One of their most memorable roles in the First World War was to carry the wounded from the front. At Gallipoli (Turkey), one man immortalised this act: John Simpson Kirkpatrick. Commonly referred to as 'Simpson and his donkey', for a little over three weeks he used a series of donkeys to carry the wounded to safety, before being mortally wounded by the enemy. The actions of Simpson and his donkey call to mind Christ's entry into Jerusalem. Simpson's voluntary self-sacrifice mirrored that of Christ, just as the biblical and ANZAC asses conveyed salvation.[10] Although Simpson was not the only soldier to use donkeys to rescue the injured, he has formed part of ANZAC legend and is commemorated across Australia.[11] Physical memorials to Simpson and his donkey are permanent reminders of emotional responses to human–animal relationships in war (Illustration 7).

One way that people's emotional associations concentrate on the ass today is through donkey welfare. In many countries, members of the public can visit donkey sanctuaries

Illustration 7: Wallace Anderson (sculptor), *The Man with the Donkey*, 1935, Shrine of Remembrance Collection, Melbourne. Photograph by the author, 2019.

and spend time volunteering and interacting with rescued donkeys. Larger sanctuaries also run global welfare projects and emergency disaster relief to improve the conditions and care of donkeys around the world. As most sanctuaries are charitable organisations, they rely on public funding to operate. In 2003, a British donkey sanctuary was reported to have received thirteen million pounds in donations, a testament to the human–animal bond that people have with donkeys.[12] Riding donkeys at the seaside is another way that many children develop an emotional bond with the humble beast of burden.[13] Books also emphasise human–animal bonds with the ass. Noel Barr's story of Ned, a lonely donkey, tells of a friendship between a lonely boy and donkey. The lonesome

Ned tries very hard to find some company – other animals reject him because they already have their friendship and kin groups, and humans exploit him for his beast of burden attributes. Timothy, however finds companionship with Ned that is mutually reciprocated.[14] Although a work of fiction, this story reinforces the human–donkey bond that some children in the world experience daily. In the book *Donkeys Can't Fly on Planes*, South Sudanese children tell stories from their time as refugees.[15] The lead story tells of a donkey, Stephen, who helped carry water and was a source of comfort and emotional support to the author during a time of trauma. The title betrays the emotional bond that the raconteur developed with the donkey: it had to stay in the refugee camp, whilst they travelled to a haven, yet nonetheless, they fondly and nostalgically remembered the donkey's contribution to their well-being.

CONCLUSION

The ass has a long history as a versatile beast. When it metaphorically plodded into medieval Europe, it was already burdened with a reputation that had been established in the ancient world by the Roman and Greek naturalists, philosophers and fablers. Medieval authors further developed their appreciation for the ass that reflected their Christian world: the ass remained stubborn and hard-working, but it also became a humble and virtuous beast. Medieval authors used it to educate, to entertain and to censure; they also politicised, sexualised, gendered and sacralised the ass. Over the medieval millennium, the ass made its mark on medieval society through its presence in the natural, religious, philosophical and literary worlds. That presence is still felt today. As the ass travelled out of the medieval world into the New World and beyond, its medieval impressions persisted. In the natural environment, people continue to benefit from the ass's beast of burden abilities; in the Christian world, the ass plays its critical role in the story of the Christ's life each Christmas and Easter. In the scholastic world, academics might no longer publicly call their adversaries an ass, but in the early twentieth century, some schoolchildren had to wear the 'donkey hat' to denote their inability to learn at the same rate as their peers.[16] As for the fictional ass, it continues to make its mark through various forms of media – book, film, cartoon – upholding its paradoxical reputation: Shrek's Donkey was hyperactive, witty and upbeat, whereas Winnie the Pooh's friend Eeyore lacked motivation, was melancholic and glum. That the medieval ass and its associated attributes have endured into the modern world emphasises a continuing theme of human–ass relationships and mutual reciprocity. The medieval ass lives on.

ENDNOTES

INTRODUCTION

1. The domestic ass (*Equus africanus asinus*) that appeared in the medieval world was a descendant from two subspecies of wild ass originating in north Africa and the Near and Middle East: the Nubian and Somalian wild asses, respectively (*Equus africanus africanus* and *Equus africanus somaliensis*). Stine Rossel et al., 'Domestication of the Donkey: Timing, Processes, and Indicators', *Proceedings of the National Academy of Sciences of the USA*, 105/10 (2008), 3716.

2. Isidore of Seville, *The Etymologies of Isidore of Seville*, ed. and tr. Stephen A. Barney et al., with the collaboration of Muriel Hall (Cambridge: Cambridge University Press, 2006).

3. Isidore, *Etymologies*, p. 249.

4. John C. Coldewey, 'Secrets of God's Creatures: Talking Animals in Medieval Drama', *European Medieval Drama*, 3 (2000), 74.

5. For the etymology of 'donkey' and 'dun (adj.)', see *The Oxford English Dictionary Online* (Oxford: Oxford University Press, 2000–), available at *http://www.oed.com*, accessed 15 August 2019.

6. Jill Mann (ed. and tr.), *Ysengrimus* (Leiden: Brill, 1987), pp. 334–7.

7. Mann, *Ysengrimus*, p. 337; Jean. R. Scheidegger, 'Le Conflit des Langues: Ecriture et Fiction dans l'Ysengrimus', *Canadian*

Journal of Netherlandic Studies, 4/1 (1983), 9–17; L. G. Donovan, 'Ysengrimus and the Early *Roman de Renard*', *Canadian Journal of Netherlandic Studies*, 4/1 (1983), 33–8.

8. Mann, *Ysengrimus*, pp. 364–5.

9. Tony Fairman, 'How the Ass became a Donkey', *English Today*, 40/4 (1994), 29–35.

10. A. E. Housman, 'The Latin for Ass', *The Classical Quarterly*, 24/1 (1930), 11–13; for the etymology of *si* and *anus* see Charlton T. Lewis and Charles Short (eds), *A Latin Dictionary* (Oxford: Clarendon Press, 1879; repr. 1958), pp. 134, 1688–9.

11. The earliest evidence for ass domestication is witnessed in visual and archaeological sources. Juliet Clutton-Brock, *Horse Power: A History of the Horse and Donkey in Human Societies* (London: Natural History Museum Publications, 1992), p. 11; Caroline Grigson, 'Size Matters: Donkeys and Horses in the Prehistory of the Southernmost Levant', *Paléorient*, 38/1–2 (2012), 189.

12. Peter Mitchell, *The Donkey in Human History: An Archaeological Perspective* (Oxford; Oxford University Press, 2018), pp. 42–4.

13. For Zimri-Lim see Jack M. Sasson, 'Thoughts of Zimri-Lim', *Biblical Archaeologist*, 47/2 (1984), 118–19; for Damascus asses, see Clutton-Brock, *Horse Power*, p. 94; for ass-riding gods, see Laura Hobgood-Oster, *Holy Dogs and Asses: Animals in the Christian Tradition* (Urbana: University of Illinois Press, 2008), pp. 26–7.

THE NATURAL WORLD OF THE ASS

1. Understandably speculative, there is some thought that some societies considered humans riding equids composite beasts. Peter Costello, *The Magic Zoo: The Natural History of Fabulous Animals* (New York: St Martin's Press, 1979), p. 60; Anthony Dent, *Donkey: The Story of the Ass from East to West* (London: Harrap and Co., 1972), p. 49.

2. Isidore of Seville, *The Etymologies of Isidore of Seville*, ed. and tr. Stephen A. Barney et al., with the collaboration of Muriel Hall (Cambridge: Cambridge University Press, 2006), p. 246.

3. Isidore, *Etymologies*, p. 11.

4. For the Latin see Isidore of Seville, *Etymologiarum sive originum libri XX*, annot. W. M. Lindsay, 2 vols (Oxford: Clarendon Press, 1962), ii, Book XII: i, 38; Isidore, *Etymologies*, p. 249.

5. In late Latin, *sedere*, when applied to animals, came to mean 'to sit on a horse; to be mounted or ridden'. Charlton T. Lewis and Charles Short (eds), *A Latin Dictionary* (Oxford: Clarendon Press, 1879; repr. 1958), p. 1158.

6. Bede (*De natura rerum*, 703); Rabanus Maurus (*De rerum naturis*, 742–7); Lambert of Saint Omer (*Liber Floridus*, 1090–1120); Hugh of Fouilly (*De avibus*, 1132–52); Alexander Neckam (*De naturis rerum*, *c.* late twelfth century).

7. Pauline Aiken, 'The Animal History of Albertus Magnus and Thomas of Cantimpré', *Speculum*, 22/2 (1947), 205–25.

8. William Wallace, 'Albertus Magnus on Suppositional Necessity in the Natural Sciences', in James A. Weisheipel (ed.), *Albertus Magnus and the Sciences: Commemorative Essays 1980* (Toronto: Pontifical Institute of Mediaeval Studies, 1980), p. 128.

9. Galen (AD 130–210) was a Greek physician who promoted the theory of Humorism. This held that four principal bodily fluids, known as humours (black and yellow bile, blood and phlegm) needed to be balanced for good health. Humorism influenced Western medicine for over 1,000 years.

10. For example, Jacob van Maerlant translated Thomas's text into Dutch, as *Der naturen bloeme* (*c.*1250), and Konrad of Megenberg's *Das Buch der Natur* (*c.*1350) was the first German-language natural history text.

11. This is often referred to as the donkey seat and it is still used today in certain parts of the world as the preferred means to ride an ass. Juliet Clutton-Brock, *Animals as Domesticates: A World View*

through History (East Lansing: Michigan State University Press, 2012), p. 31.

12. Thomas Cantimpratensis, *Liber de natura rerum* (New York: Walter de Gruyter, 1973), p. 109; the ass's dorsal cross is a vestige of earlier striped ass species that can be traced back to the zebra on the equid cladogram. Dent, *East to West*, p. 19.

13. All quotes from and references to the Bible in English are from the critical scholarly edition of the *King James Version* (KJV), available at *https://www.academic-bible.com*, accessed 15 August 2019.

14. 'En effet le bestiaire n'est pas pour fonction première d'observer les animaux en eux-mêmes: les animaux y sont un point de départ, ou plutôt un prétexte, pour permettre à l'homme de se connaître.' Bruno Roy, 'La Belle e(s)t la Bête: Aspects du Bestiaire Féminin au Moyen Age', *Etudes Françaises*, 10/3 (1974), 319–20.

15. For a thorough and convincing discussion of the *Physiologus*'s date of production, see Alan Scott, 'The Date of the *Physiologus*', *Vigiliae Christianae*, 52/4 (1998), 430–41.

16. Jonathan Morton, 'The Book of the World at an Anglo-Norman Court: The Bestiaire de Philippe de Thaon as a Theological Performance', in Laura Ashe, Wendy Scase and David Lawton (eds), *New Medieval Literatures*, 16 (Woodbridge: Boydell and Brewer, 2016), p. 5; P. T. Eden (ed. and tr.), *Theobaldi 'Physiologus'* (Leiden: Brill, 1972), pp. 2–3.

17. Willene B. Clark, *A Medieval Book of Beasts: The Second-Family Bestiary: Commentary, Art, Text and Translation* (Woodbridge: Boydell and Brewer, 2006), pp. 9, 98–99.

18. The *Physiologus* did not feature domesticated animals. Michael J. Curley (ed. and tr.), *Physiologus* (Austin: University of Texas Press, 1979), p. 15.

19. Friedrich Ohly, *Sensus Spiritualis: Studies in Medieval Significance and the Philology of Culture*, ed. Samuel P. Jaffe, tr. Kenneth J. Northcott

(Chicago: University of Chicago Press, 2005), p. 2; Henri de Lubac, *Exégèse Médiévale: Les Quatre Sens de L'Ecriture* (Paris: Aubier, 1959), pp. 571–86.

20. T. H. White, *The Book of Beasts: Being a Translation from a Latin Bestiary of the Twelfth Century* (London: Cape, 1969), p. 82; Cambridge University Library, MS Li.4.26 f.25r, available at *https://cudl.lib.cam.ac.uk/view/MS-II-00004-00026/77#*, accessed 11 December 2019; Richard Barber (tr.), *Bestiary: Being an English version of the Bodleian Library Oxford* M. S. *Bodley 764* (Woodbridge: Boydell Press, 1993), p. 97; Bodleian Library MS, Bodl. 764 f.44r, available at *https://digital.bodleian.ox.ac.uk/inquire/p/861b32a3-19f7-41e7-961d-e774727708f6*, accessed 11 December 2019.

21. Thomas Cantimpratensis, *Liber de natura rerum*, p. 148.

22. Albertus Magnus, *On Animals: A Medieval Summa Zoologica*, ed. and tr. Kenneth F. Kitchell, Jr., and Irven M. Resnick (Baltimore: Johns Hopkins University Press, 1999), pp. 1231–3, 1521.

23. Albertus Magnus, *On Animals*, pp. 1450–1.

24. Thomas Cantimpratensis, *Liber de natura rerum*, p. 155.

25. Theodore John Rivers (tr.), *Laws of the Alamans and Bavarians* (Philadelphia: University of Pennsylvania Press, 1977), p. 137.

26. Albert Leighton, *Transport and Communication in Early Medieval Europe* AD 500–1100 (Newton Abbot: David and Charles, 1972), pp. 63–4.

27. Ian Baxter, 'A Donkey (*Equus asinus* L.) Partial Skeleton from a Mid–Late Anglo-Saxon Alluvial Layer at Deans Yard Westminster, London SW1', *Environmental Archaeology*, 7/1 (2002), 89–94. Similar limited finds from other ports in regions above the 50-degree latitude have also been uncovered (Hedeby, Denmark, and Dorestad, the Netherlands), suggesting small numbers of asses in some colder climates, most likely used in specific locations as beasts of burden transporting import and export goods.

28. John Langdon, *Horses, Oxen and Technological Innovation: The Use of Draught Animals in English Farming from* 1066–1500 (Cambridge: Cambridge University Press, 1986), pp 40–2, 50; Dent, *East to West*, p. 58.

29. Langdon, *Horses, Oxen and Technological Innovation*, pp. 28–9, 294.

30. Benoit Clavel and Jean-Hervé Yvinec, 'L'Archéozoologie du Moyen Age au Début de la Période Moderne dans la Moitié Nord de la France', in Jean Chapelot (ed.), *Trente Ans d'Archéologie Médiévale en France: Un Bilan pour un Avenir* (Caen: Publications de CRAHM, 2010), p. 76.

31. Pierre Caillat and Yan Laborie, 'Approche de l'Alimentation Carnée des Occupants du Castrum d'Auberoche (Dordogne) d'après les Données de l'Archéozoologie', *Archéologie du Midi Médiéval*, 15/16 (1997), 165, 174–5.

32. Rosamond Faith, 'Farms and Families in Ninth-Century Provence', *Early Medieval Europe*, 18/2 (2010), 187.

33. I would like to thank Dr Elvis Mallorquí from the University of Girona for generously providing this information.

34. Sándor Bökönyi, 'The Development of Stockbreeding and Herding in Medieval Europe', in Del Sweeney (ed.), *Agriculture in the Middle Ages: Technology, Practice and Representation* (Philadelphia: University of Philadelphia Press, 1995), pp. 50–1.

35. Joseph Gies and Frances Gies, *Merchants and Moneymen: The Commercial Revolution*, 1000–1500 (New York; Crowell, 1972), p. 81.

36. Thomas of Cantimpré wrote: '[P]ontem transituri asini, si per medium fluvium vident, de facili non transeunt'. *Liber de natura rerum*, p. 109.

37. John Clark (ed.), *The Medieval Horse and its Equipment c.*1150–*c.*1450 (Woodbridge: Boydell Press, 2004), pp. 76–8.

38. Jean-Bernard Y. D. Dereclenne, 'Le Prieure de Sainte-Sigolène, lieu-dit Troclar à Lagrave (Tarn): Etude Archéozoologique des Vestiges Osseux des IX–XIIIè siècles (Fouilles 1993–5)'

(unpublished PhD thesis, Université Paul-Sabatier de Toulouse, Toulouse, 2001), p. 64.

39. Albertus Magnus, *On Animals*, p. 1451.

40. Priscilla Throop (tr.), *Hildegard von Bingen's Physica: The Complete English Translation of her Classic Work on Health and Healing* (Rochester, VT: Healing Arts Press, 1998), p. 212.

41. There is strong evidence across southern France and Italy for ass meat consumption. V. Forest, 'Alimentation Carnée dans le Languedoc Mediéval (Les témoignages archéozoologiques des vertébrés supérieurs)', *Archéologie du Midi Médiéval*, 15/16 (1997), 141–60; Paul Arthur et al., '"Masseria Quattro Macine" – A Deserted Medieval Village and Its Territory in Southern Apulia: An Interim Report on Field Survey, Excavation and Document Analysis', *Papers of the British School at Rome*, 64 (1996), 222.

42. Peter Mitchell, *The Donkey in Human History: An Archaeological Perspective* (Oxford; Oxford University Press, 2018), pp. 165–6.

43. Rosalind Hill (ed.), *The Deeds of the Franks and the Other Pilgrims to Jerusalem* (Edinburgh: Thomas Nelson and Sons, 1962), p. 57; Fulcher of Chartres, *Chronicle of the First Crusade*, tr. Martha E. McGinty (Philadelphia: University of Pennsylvania Press, 1941), pp. 56, 77.

44. Peter Tudebode, *Historia de Hierosolymitano Itinere*, tr. John H. Hill and Laurita L. Hill (Philadelphia: American Philosophical Society, 1974), p. 80.

45. Carol Sweetenham, 'What Really Happened to Eurvin de Creel's Donkey? Anecdotes in Sources for the First Crusade', in Marcus Bull and Damien Kempf (eds), *Writing the Early Crusades: Text, Transmission and Memory* (Woodbridge, Suffolk; Rochester, NY: Boydell and Brewer, 2014), pp. 75–88.

46. Fulcher of Chartres, *Chronicle of the First Crusade*, p. 44.

47. Robert S. Lopez, *The Commercial Revolution of the Middle Ages 950–1350* (Cambridge: Cambridge University Press, 1976), p. 46.

48. Joyce E. Salisbury, *The Beast Within: Animals in the Middle Ages* (New York; Routledge, 1994), pp. 32–6.

49. Rivers, *Laws of the Alamans and Bavarians*, p. 37.

50. Albert of Aachen, *Historia Ierosolimitana: History of the Journey to Jerusalem*, ed. and tr. Susan B. Edgington (Oxford: Clarendon Press, 2007), Bk IV: 54, pp. 332–3.

51. Albert of Aachen, *Historia Ierosolimitana*, Bk IV: 54–5, pp. 332–5.

52. Albert of Aachen, *Historia Ierosolimitana*, Bk IV: 34, pp. 300–1.

53. Katherine Fischer Drew, *The Laws of the Salian Franks* (Philadelphia; University of Pennsylvania Press, 1991), pp 99, 205.

54. The Truce of God (1027), was an extension of the Peace of God (989) – two Church-driven movements to restrict violence within Western Christendom resulting from the decline of the Carolingian empire. Donald J. Kagay, 'The Usatges of Barcelona: The Fundamental Law of Catalonia', *The Library of Iberian Resources Online*, p. 109, available at *file:///C:/Users/smkl/Downloads/Kagay%20-%20law%20and%20Catalonia.pdf*, accessed 15 August 2019.

55. Gregory of Tours, *History of the Franks*, Book X, available at *http://thuleitalia.org/Nordica/Gregory%20of%20Tours%20%20History%20of%20the%20Franks.htm#book*10, accessed 15 August 2019; Norman Cohn, *The Pursuit of the Millennium: Revolutionary Millenarians and Mystical Anarchists of the Middle Ages* (New York: Oxford University Press, 1970), p. 62.

56. Nathaniel Lane Taylor, 'The Will and Society in Medieval Catalonia and Languedoc, 800–1200' (unpublished PhD thesis, Harvard University, Cambridge, MA, 1995), p. 198.

THE RELIGIOUS ASS

1. All quotes from and references to the Bible in English are from the critical scholarly edition of the King James Version (KJV), available at *https://www.academic-bible.com*, accessed 15 August 2019; although the ass is ubiquitous in biblical imagery of the Nativity and the Holy Family's flight into Egypt, the Gospels do

not mention the beast of burden. However, it is noted in the apocryphal Gospels of James (17: 2–3) and the Pseudo-Matthew (13: 1–2), respectively. Bart D. Ehrman and Zlatko Pleše ed. and tr., *The Other Gospels: Accounts of Jesus from Outside the New Testament* (New York: Oxford University Press, 2014), pp. 32, 50; for the Gospel entries on Christ's Palm Sunday triumphal procession into Jerusalem, see Matt. 21: 1–11, Mark 11: 1–11, Luke 19: 29–44, and John 12: 12–19.

2. Matt. 21: 1–5; Mark 11: 1–10; Luke 19: 29–35; John 12: 12–15.

3. For a more detailed list of biblical asses as beasts of burden, see Kenneth C. Way, *Donkeys in the Biblical World: Ceremony and Symbol* (Winona Lake, IN: Eisenbrauns, 2011), p. 170.

4. Albert Pauphilet (ed.), *La Queste del Saint Graal* (Paris: Champion, 1949), p. 158.

5. Robert Alter, 'Balaam and the Ass', *The Kenyon Review*, 26/4 (2004), 7.

6. The quote from Origen's homily 14, 4 can be found in Migne, *PG*, 12, 683A. Cited in J. R. Baskin, 'Origen on Balaam: The Dilemma of the Unworthy Prophet', *Vigiliae Christianae*, 37/1 (1983), p. 28, n.41.

7. Quote from Origen's homily 13, 8 (*PG*, 12, 676B), cited in Baskin, 'Origen on Balaam', p.28, n.42.

8. Sandra Billington, 'The Cheval Fol of Lyon and Other Asses', in Clifford Davidson (ed.), *Fools and Folly* (Kalamazoo: Medieval Institute Publication, 1996), p. 9.

9. Despite interactions between the three monotheistic faiths – Christianity, Judaism, Islam – overall, medieval society was not a tolerant or pluralist society and there is ample evidence of anti-Jewish sentiment throughout the period. Although some bestiary texts could be read as anti-Jewish, arguably the message to be taken from such texts was the importance of being within the Church (Christian) as God was the ultimate judge. John C. Jacobs (tr. and ed.), *The Fables of Odo of Cheriton* (New York: Syracuse University Press, 1985), p. 23–4. For a fuller discussion

on how medieval anti-Jewish sentiment differs from modern expressions and understanding of antisemitism, see Adams and Hess's introduction to *The Medieval Roots of Antisemitism*. Jonathan Adams and Cordelia Hess, 'Volcanic Archives: Towards a Direct Comparison of Pre–Modern and Modern Forms of Antisemitism', in Jonathan Adams and Cordelia Hess (eds), *The Medieval Roots of Antisemitism: Continuities and Discontinuities from the Middle Ages to the Present Day* (London: Routledge, 2018), pp. 3–16.

10. Gabriel Bianciotto (ed.), *Bestiaires du Moyen Age* (Paris: Editions Stock, 1980), p. 101.

11. Richard Barber (tr.), *Bestiary: Being an English Version of the Bodleian Library, Oxford M.S. Bodley 764* (Woodbridge: Boydell Press, 1993), p. 97; Bodleian Library MS, Bodl. 764 fos 44r and 44v, available at *https://digital.bodleian.ox.ac.uk/inquire/p/861b32a3-19f7-41e7-961d-e774727708f6*, accessed 11 December 2019.

12. Barber, *Bestiary*, p. 98.

13. This complex verse is open to several interpretations, e.g. the Christian narrative of redemption, but medieval authors did not restrict themselves to a single meaning – animals offered myriad ways to show God's teachings. Dongmyung Ahn, 'Beastly yet Lofty Burdens: The Donkey and the Subdeacon in the Middle Ages', in Irène Fabry-Tehranch and Anna Russakoff (eds), *L'Humain et l'Animal dans la France Médiévale (XIIe–XVe s.)* (Amsterdam: Rodopi, 2014), p. 153.

14. Bodleian Library MS, Bodl. 764 fos 44r and 44v, available at *https://digital.bodleian.ox.ac.uk/inquire/p/861b32a3-19f7-41e7-961d-e774727708f6*, accessed 11 December 2019.

15. Jacobs, *The Fables of Odo of Cheriton*, p. 23–4.

16. Philippe de Thaün, *Le Bestiaire*, ed. Emmanuel Walberg (Geneva: Slatkine, 1970).

17. Philippe de Thaün, *Le Bestiaire*, p. 4, lines 79–90; my translation, based on Thomas Wright's parallel translation in *The Bestiary of Philippe de Thaon*, ed. and tr. Thomas Wright (London: The

Historical Society, 1841), p. 8, lines 39–44, available at
*http://bestiary.ca/etexts/wright1841/bestiary%20of%20philippe%20de%20
thaon%20-%20wright%20-%20parallel%20text.pdf*, accessed
15 August 2019.

18. Heiko A. Oberman, 'The Stubborn Jews: Timing the Escalation
of Antisemitism in Late Medieval Europe', *Leo Baeck Institute Year
Book*, 34 (1989), xi–xxv.

19. For an overview of medieval Christian attitudes towards and
interactions with Jews see Robert Chazan, *The Jews of Medieval
Western Christendom*, 1000–1500 (Cambridge: Cambridge
University Press, 2006).

20. Ursula Schlegel, 'The Christchild as Devotional Image in
Medieval Italian Sculpture: A Contribution to Ambrogio
Lorenzetti Studies', *The Art Bulletin*, 52/1 (1970), 8, 10.

21. Thomas Ramey Watson, 'St. Francis' "Brother Ass" and Wyatt's
"Ye Old Mule"', *American Notes and Queries*, 19 (1981), 71; Norman
Hammond, 'Bellini's Ass: A Note on the Frick "St Francis"',
The Burlington Magazine, 144/1186 (2002), 24–6.

22. For Bellini's painting in the Frick Collection, New York, see
Giovanni Bellini, *St. Francis in the Desert* (*c*.1480), The Frick
Collection, available at *https://www.frick.org/exhibitions/past/2011/
bellini*, accessed 15 August 2019.

23. This tale is recorded in a late fourth-century text, *Historia
Monachorum in Aegypto* which can be found in Helen Waddell (tr.),
Beasts and Saints (London: Constable, 1946), p. 19.

24. Waddell, *Beasts and Saints*, pp. 30–8.

25. Pamela Sheingorn (tr.), *The Book of Sainte Foy* (Philadelphia:
University of Pennsylvania Press, 1995), pp. 56–8, 104–5, 207–10.

26. Animal resurrection was virtually unknown in the patristic
tradition; its potential genesis dates from the seventh- to
eighth-century Irish hagiographic tradition. Also, animal
resurrections usually occurred from the gathering of the animal's
skin and bones once the beast had been eaten. Dominic

Alexander, *Saints and Animals* (Woodbridge: Boydell Press, 2008), pp. 84, 107.

27. Sheingorn, *The Book of Sainte Foy*, pp. 104–5.

28. Elizabeth Lipsmeyer, 'Devotion and Decorum: Intention and Quality in Medieval German Sculpture', *Gesta*, 34/1 (1995), 22.

29. Lipsmeyer, 'Devotion and Decorum', 24.

30. The Feast of Fools was particularly prevalent in northern France, with records of its practice dating from the early twelfth century. Max Harris, *Sacred Folly: A New History of the Feast of Fools* (Ithaca, NY: Cornell University Press, 2011), p. 6.

31. Ongoing scholarship tends to posit the Feast of Fools as a bowdlerised ritual that attracted censure. It is becoming more apparent that this interpretation is problematic. Certainly, in the fifteenth century papal, royal and scholastic authorities censured and prohibited the festival, but the earliest evidence from the twelfth century points to an accepted solemn church ritual. For a full discussion on the confusion, see Harris, *Sacred Folly*, esp. prologue and chapters 6 and 7.

32. Ahn, 'Beastly yet Lofty Burdens', 150.

33. Ahn, 'Beastly yet Lofty Burdens', 145.

34. Subdeacons had an uncertain place in the clerical hierarchy that was not codified until 1207, when they were deemed to be the most junior of the higher order of clerics, having been elevated from the lower orders. Harris, *Sacred Folly*, p. 67; Roger E. Reynolds, 'The Subdiaconate as a Sacred and Superior Order', in *Clerics in the Early Middle Ages: Hierarchy and Image*, Variorum Collected Studies Series, CS669 (Aldershot: Ashgate, 1999), iv, p. 1.

35. The term emotion is a modern construct – *passio* (s.), *passiones* (pl.); *affectio* (s.), *affectiones* (pl.). Thomas Dixon, *From Passions to Emotions: The Creation of a Secular Psychological Category* (Cambridge: Cambridge University Press, 2003), pp. 4, 39–40.

36. Sainte Foy's reliquary, elaborately decorated with many precious stones, attests to her saintly potency.

37. This practice emerged around the beginning of the twelfth century and was epitomised in Anselm of Canterbury's orations. Sarah McNamer, *Affective Meditation and the Invention of Medieval Compassion* (Philadelphia: University of Pennsylvania Press, 2010).

38. Cited in Jeanette Beer, *Beasts of Love: Richard de Fournival's* Bestiaire d'amour *and a Woman's Response* (Toronto: University of Toronto Press, 2003), p. 3.

39. Nancy M. Martin and Joseph Runzo, 'Love', in John Corrigan (ed.), *The Oxford Handbook of Religion and Emotion* (Oxford: Oxford University Press, 2008), p. 310.

40. In the case of affective piety, the relationship is between participant and performer. Julian Hanich, 'Collective Viewing: The Cinema and Affective Audience Interrelations', *Passions in Context: The International Journal for History and Theory of Emotions*, 1 (2010), 3.

41. Hanich, 'Collective Viewing'.

THE SCHOLASTIC ASS

1. Jean Leclercq, *The Love of Learning and the Desire for God: A Study of Monastic Culture*, tr. Catharine Mirashi (New York: Fordham University Press, 1988), pp. 1–3.

2. Charles H. Haskins, *The Renaissance of the Twelfth Century* (Cambridge: Harvard University Press, 1939), p. 5.

3. Leclercq, *The Love of Learning*, p. 2.

4. Maureen A. Tilley, 'Martyrs, Monks, Insects and Animals', in Joyce E. Salisbury (ed.), *The Medieval World of Nature* (New York: Garland, 1993), p. 97.

5. Saint Augustine, *The Literal Meaning of Genesis*, tr. John Hammond Taylor (New York: Newman Press, 1982), p. 193.

6. Thomas Aquinas, *The 'Summa theologica' of St. Thomas Aquinas*, tr. Fathers of the English Dominican Province (Getzville, NY: William S. Hein., 2014), p. 31, I, Q. 3, Art. 1.

7. For the non-specialist in philosophical debates and further explanations of universals, particulars, realist and nominalist

schools, see Jens Tomas Anfindsen, 'On Particulars and Universals', HonestThinking.org, available at *http://www.honest thinking.org/en/pub/*HT.2005.JTA.*Particulars_and_universals.html*, accessed 15 August 2019.

8. James N. Jordan, *Western Philosophy: From Antiquity to the Middle Ages* (New York: Macmillan, 1987), p. 333; for a simple but more expansive explanation see Virginie Greene, *Logical Fictions in Medieval Literature and Philosophy* (Cambridge: Cambridge University Press, 2014), pp. 15–19.

9. I have used Spade's simplified explanation as outlined in his introduction. Paul V. Spade (ed. and tr.), *Five Texts on the Medieval Problem of Universals: Porphyry, Boethius, Abelard, Duns Scotus, Ockham* (Indianapolis: Hackett Publishing, 1994), p. vii.

10. Timothy Ernst, 'Quidam homo est asinus: The Originality and Influence of Peter Abelard upon Medieval Thought' (unpublished MA thesis, University of Louisville, Louisville, 2011), p. 61.

11. Ernst, 'Quidam homo est asinus', p. 61.

12. Abelard was more nominalist than realist in his thought, although the nominalist concept was not fully developed until later by William Ockham.

13. Greene, *Logical Fictions*, pp. 17–19.

14. Nominalists do better here, because they claim reality lies in the particular only. So Brunellus and Socrates are different because they have different instantiation of particular matter. However, for Nominalists the general term *animal* is only nominal, the animal as such has no reality.

15. Aquinas, *Summa Theologica*, pp. 181–2, Q. 15, Art. 2.; Peter G. Sobol, 'The Shadow of Reason: Explanations of Intelligent Animal Behavior in the Thirteenth Century', in Joyce E. Salisbury (ed.), *The Medieval World of Nature: A Book of Essays* (London, New York: Garland Publishing, 1993), p. 109. Sobol says that as the scholastics studied animals more closely, they became less certain about the definitive divide.

16. Thomas Cantimpratensis, *Liber de natura rerum* (New York: Walter de Gruyter, 1973), p. 108.

17. Nicholas Rescher, *Scholastic Meditations* (Washington, DC: The Catholic University of America Press, 2005), pp. 4–5.

18. Rescher, *Scholastic Meditations*, pp. 5–6; Ruth Weintraub, 'What can we Learn from Buridan's Ass?', *Canadian Journal of Philosophy*, 42/3–4 (2012), 283.

19. Rescher, *Scholastic Meditations*, pp. 5–6.

20. Aquinas, *Summa Theologica*, p. 168, I–II, Q. 13, Art. 6.

21. Rescher, *Scholastic Meditations*, p. 20.

22. William of Ockham, *Opera Philosophica* IV, cited in Rescher, *Scholastic Meditations*, p. 18.

23. William of Ockham, *Opera Philosophica* IV, cited in Sharon M. Kaye, 'Why the Liberty of Indifference is Worth Wanting: Buridan's Ass, Friendship, and Peter John Olivi', *History of Philosophy Quarterly*, 21/1 (2004), 24.

24. William of Ockham, *Quodlibetal Questions*, tr. Alfred J. Freddoso and Francis E. Kelly, 2 vols (New Haven: Yale University Press, 1991), i, p. 142, Second quodlibet, Q. 13.

25. Kaye, 'Why the Liberty of Indifference is Worth Wanting', 24, n.4.

26. Edward Grant, *God and Reason in the Middle Ages* (New York: Cambridge University Press, 2001), p. 125.

27. Helen Adolf, 'The Ass and the Harp', *Speculum*, 25/1 (1950), 49–57; Laura Cleaver, *Education in Twelfth-Century Art and Architecture: Images of Learning in Europe, c.*1100–1220 (Woodbridge: Boydell and Brewer, 2016), pp. 63–83.

28. Boethius, *The Consolation of Philosophy*, tr. Victor Watts (London: Penguin, 1999), p. 9.

29. Peter Biller, 'Intellectuals and the Masses: Oxen and She-asses in the Medieval Church', in John H. Arnold (ed.), *The Oxford Handbook of Medieval Christianity* (Oxford: Oxford University Press, 2014), p. 324.

30. William of Auxerre, *Summa aurea*, ed. Jean Ribaillier, 4 vols (Paris: CNRS, 1980–7), i, p. 212.

31. Laura Cleaver, 'Disorder in Nature: The Example of the Ass and Harp in Twelfth-Century Manuscripts', in Laura Cleaver, Kathryn Gerry and Jim Harris (eds), *Art and Nature: Studies in Medieval Art and Architecture* (London: Courtauld Institute of Art, 2009), pp. 131–42.

32. John of Salisbury, *The Metalogicon of John of Salisbury: A Twelfth-Century Defense of the Verbal and Logical Arts of the Trivium*, tr. Daniel D. McGarry (Berkeley: University of California Press, 1962), p. 13.

33. Terrance Callan, 'Comparison of Humans to Animals in 2 Peter 2, 10b–22', *Biblica*, 90/1 (2009), 101–13.

34. 'Quasi enim asinus est ad lyram lector librum tenens, id ad quod liber est factus agere non valens', Peter Abelard, 'Epistola 8', in Migne (ed.), *PL*, clxxviii, col. 310.

35. Grant, *God and Reason*, p. 3.

THE ASS IN LITERATURE

1. '[T]out est didacticisme au Moyen Age.' Pierre-Yves Badel, *Introduction à la Vie Littéraire du Moyen Age* (Paris: Bordas, 1984), p. 165.

2. Joseph Bédier, *Les Fabliaux: Etudes de Littérature Populaire et d'Histoire Littéraire du Moyen Age* (2nd edn, Emile Bouillon: Paris, 1895), p. 30.

3. Willem Noomen (ed.), *NRCF*, 10 vols (Assen: Van Gorcum, 1994), viii: 207–14, line 51.

4. Lorcin notes the conservatism of the fabliaux; Marie-Thérèse Lorcin, *Façons de Sentir et de Penser: Les Fabliaux Français* (Paris: Champion, 1979), p. 42; Odo of Cheriton, a preacher and fabulist, also championed the status quo, using fables to satirise the Church and high-ranking ecclesiastics. John C. Jacobs (ed. and tr.), *The Fables of Odo of Cheriton* (New York: Syracuse University Press, 1985).

5. Marie de France, *Fables*, ed. and tr. Harriet Spiegel (Toronto: University of Toronto Press, 1987), pp. 9–10; Mary Lou Martin, *The Fables of Marie de France: An English Translation* (Birmingham, AL: Summa Publications, 1984), p. 5.

6. Noomen, *NRCF*, ix, pp. 237–50.

7. Laurent Jégou, 'La Sépulture de l'Ane. Le Sort Réservé aux Corps des Excommuniés d'après les Sources Ecrites et Archéologiques (IXe–XIe siècles)', in G. Bührer-Thierry and S. Gioanni (eds), *Exclure de la Communauté Chrétienne: Sens et Pratiques Sociales de l'Anathème et de L'Excommunication (IVe-XIIe siècles)* (Turnhout: Brepols, 2015), pp. 197–212.

8. Laughter is socially contagious and promotes a sense of social cohesion. Martha Bayless, 'Laughter in a Deadly Context: *Le Sacristain, Maldon*, Troilus, Merlin', in Per Förnegård et al. (eds), *Tears, Sighs and Laughter: Expressions of Emotions in the Middle Ages* (Stockholm: Kungl, 2017), pp. 153.

9. Mary E. Leech, 'That's Not Funny: Comic Forms, Didactic Purpose, and Physical Injury in Medieval Comic tales', *LATCH*, 1 (2008), 105.

10. David Rollo, *Glamorous Sorcery: Magic and Literacy in the High Middle Ages* (Minneapolis: University of Minnesota Press, 2000), esp. chapters 2 and 5.

11. Glynnis M. Cropp and Alison Hanham, 'Richard II from Donkey to Royal Martyr: Perceptions of Eustache Deschamps and Contemporary French Writers', *Parergon*, 24/1 (2007), 101–36.

12. Jill Mann, *From Aesop to Reynard: Beast Literature in Medieval Britain* (Oxford University Press, 2009); Diane Heath, 'Burnellus Speaks: Beast Books and Beastliness in Late Twelfth-Century Canterbury', *South Atlantic Review*, 81/2 (2016), 33–54.

13. Lines 57–8 of the *Speculum Stultorum* declare: 'Regna licet teneat sceptrumque leonis asellus / Juraque det populis, semper asellus erit' ('Although the ass holds the lion's sceptre and kingdom and gives obedience/laws to the people, it will always be an ass'). Cited in Mann, *From Aesop to Reynard*, p. 102.

14. Louise O. Vasvari, 'A Tale of "Tailing" in the *Libro de Buen Amor*', *Journal of Interdisciplinary Literary Studies*, 2 (1990), 13; Anthony J. Cárdenas-Rotunno, '(Mis)reading the "*Libro de Buen Amor*": Exemplary Ambiguity and Ambiguous Exempla', *Romance Notes*, 52/1 (2012), 3–11.

15. Cited in Louise Haywood, *Sex, Scandal, and Sermon in Fourteenth-Century Spain: Juan Ruiz's* Libro de Buen Amor (Basingstoke: Palgrave Macmillan, 2008), p. 87.

16. Bruno Roy, 'La Belle e(s)t la Bête: Aspects du Bestiaire Féminin au Moyen Age', *Etudes Françaises*, 10/3 (1974), 327–9.

17. My emphasis.

18. Cited in Haywood, *Sex, Scandal, and Sermon*, p. 88.

19. Roy, 'La Belle e(s)t la Bête', 328.

20. Giovanni Boccaccio, *The Decameron of Giovanni Boccaccio*, tr. James M. Rigg (London: Routledge, 1905), p. 68.

21. Although slightly outside the medieval parameters of this book, it merits consideration as it reveals themes pertinent to this book. It is generally considered that the 'Golden Ass' was lost to medieval audiences until towards the end of the Middle Ages, but Boccaccio was certainly familiar with Apuleius's novel. Janet Levarie Smarr, 'Review of Igor Candido, *Boccaccio Umanista: Studi su Boccaccio e Apuleio* (Ravenna: Longo Editore, 2014)', in *Renaissance Quarterly*, 68/1 (2015), 369–71.

22. Apuleius, *Metamorphoses (The Golden Ass)*, ed. and tr. J. Arthur Hanson (Cambridge, MA: Harvard University Press, 2014), Bk IX, pp. 144–7.

23. Apuleius, *Metamorphoses*, Bk X, pp. 204–5.

24. Apuleius, *Metamorphoses*, Bk X, pp. 210–1.

25. This event is not Lucius's only sexual encounter; he is also compelled to have sexual intercourse with a condemned woman, as part of her public execution before she is thrown to the beasts. Apuleius, *Metamorphoses*, Bk X, pp. 212–13, 222–3, 234–7.

26. Martin G. Eisner and Marc D. Schachter, '"Libido Sciendi": Apuleius, Boccaccio, and the Study of the History of Sexuality', *PMLA*, 124/3 (2009), 817–37.

27. The *Romulus Nilantii* were a fifth-century Latin version of Aesop's fables, based on the first-century Phaedrus's Aesop adaptations. Harriet Spiegel, 'The Male Animal in the Fables of Marie de France', in Clare A. Lees, Thelma Fenster and Jo Ann MacNamara (eds), *Medieval Masculinities: Regarding Men in the Middle Ages* (Minneapolis: University of Minnesota Press, 1994), pp. 111–26.

28. My position on gender is based on Joan Scott's now old, but still useful proposition for historical analysis: that gender is an analytic category in which gender legitimises and constructs social relationships. Here gender is understood as a fundamental aspect of social relationships based on perceived differences between the sexes and is exemplified through cultural symbols. It moves away from kinship as the basis for social organisation, preferencing other social polities such as education, economics, religion and politics. See Joan W. Scott, 'Gender: A Useful Category of Historical Analysis', *The American Historical Review*, 91/5 (1986), 1053–75, esp. 1066–70.

29. Michelle Z. Rosaldo, 'The Use and Abuse of Anthropology: Reflections on Feminism and Cross-Cultural Understanding', *Signs*, 5/3 (1980), 400.

30. Hugh of Nonant (Bishop of Coventry), 'The Longchamp Letter', in M. J. Franklin (ed.), *English Episcopal Acta: Coventry and Lichfield 1138–1208* (London: Oxford University Press, for the British Academy, 1998), xvii, p. 128.

POSTSCRIPT: THE MEDIEVAL ASS IN THE POST-MEDIEVAL ERA

1. Workshop of Lucas Cranach the Elder, 'Papal Ass', Staatliche Kunstsammlungen Dresden, available at *https://artsandculture.google.com/asset/papal-ass/fAE79ZFRTcIoSQ*, accessed 15 August 2019.

2.   Lawrence P. Buck, '"Anatomia Antichristi": Form and Content of the Papal Antichrist', *The Sixteenth Century Journal*, 42/2 (2011), 364.

3.   Nick Miller, 'It Began at the Pub: The Campaign to Shame Brexit's Biggest "Donkeys"',*The Age*, available at *https://www.theage.com.au/world/europe/it-began-at-the-pub-the-campaign-to-shame-brexits-biggest-donkeys-20190201-p50uzq.html*, accessed 15 August 2019.

4.   W. A. Rogers, 'Deliberations of Congress', Granger Collection, available at *https://en.wikipedia.org/wiki/File:Deliberations_of_Congress.jpg*, accessed 15 August 2019.

5.   Jill Bough, 'The Mirror has Two Faces: Contradictory Reflections of Donkeys in Western Literature from Lucius to Balthazar', *Animals*, 1 (2011), 61.

6.   Dan Terkla and Thomas L. Reed, Jr., '"I'm Gonna Git Medieval on Your Ass": *Pulp Fiction* for the 90s – the 1190s', *Studies in Popular Culture*, 20/1 (1997), 39–52.

7.   Anthony Dent, *Donkey: The Story of the Ass from East to West* (London: Harrap and Co., 1972), pp. 131–6.

8.   Dent, *East to West*, pp. 136–7.

9.   Jill Bough, *Donkey* (London: Reaktion, 2011), pp. 112–19.

10.   Peter Mitchell, *The Donkey in Human History: An Archaeological Perspective* (Oxford; Oxford University Press, 2018), p. 234.

11.   John Simpson Kirkpatrick was from County Durham, England, and travelled to Australia *c*.1910. He enlisted with the Australian forces as a stretcher bearer and landed at Gallipoli on 25 April 1915; he died on 19 May 1915.

12.   Tim Dowling, 'Pin the Cheque on the Donkey', *The Guardian*, available at *https://www.theguardian.com/society/2003/feb/18/animalrights.fundraising*, accessed 15 August 2019.

13.   In recent years more attention has been drawn to the ethics of this practice, especially adults riding donkeys, as well as some owners' mistreatment, or neglect, of their animals. Joanna Whitehead, 'They're Part of the British Seaside Experience, but are Donkey Rides Ethical?', *The Independent*, available at

https://www.independent.co.uk/travel/news-and-advice/donkey-rides-animal-rights-santorini-clevedon-tradition-cruelty-a8483026.html, accessed 15 August 2019. For a scholarly study, see Paul A. G. Tully and Neil Carr, 'The Oppression of Donkeys in Seaside Tourism', *International Journal of the Sociology of Leisure*, 3 (2020), 53–70.

14. Noel Barr, *Ned the Lonely Donkey: A Story for Children* (Loughborough: Wills and Hepworth, 1952).

15. Victorian Refugee Health Network, 'Donkeys can't Fly on Planes – Stories of Survival from South Sudanese Refugee Children Living in Australia', available at *https://refugeehealthnetwork.org.au/donkeys-cant-fly-on-planes-stories-of-survival-from-south-sudanese-refugee-children-living-in-australia/*, accessed 15 August 2019.

16. A donkey hat – also known as the dunce's cap – or a cap with a large letter 'D' was used to denote a child who was slow to learn, or to control disruptive behaviour through public humiliation.

FURTHER READING

There is no one leading authority on the medieval ass; however, the following texts are good points of departure for anyone wanting to study the medieval beast of burden.

Peter Mitchell, *The Donkey in Human History: An Archaeological Perspective* (Oxford: Oxford University Press, 2018): Peter Mitchell's book presents a long chronological and global history of the ass and its relationship with humans, from the prehistory era to the present day. The work is informed primarily by archaeological evidence and further supported by historical and anthropological testimony. There is one chapter dedicated to the ass in the medieval world that considers the ass in both medieval Christian and Islamic contexts. Overall, this book draws attention to the ass's importance in supporting human endeavours and advancement.

Jill Bough, *Donkey* (London: Reaktion, 2011): Jill Bough offers a cultural history of the donkey based on the beast's actual history and its many representations. This compact book offers five themed chapters – domestication, religion and mythology, colonisation, war, and creative representations

– and, like Mitchell's book, has a chronological approach. The reader must search each chapter for the medieval ass, but it is a worthwhile exercise. This is an informative book that promotes the donkey as worthy of respect and attention.

Joyce Salisbury, *The Beast Within: Animals in the Middle Ages* (London: Routledge, 1994): Joyce Salisbury's book takes a thematic approach to animals in general, not just the ass, and considers changing attitudes towards animals in the daily and imagined medieval world. She comments on the ass in all but one of her chapters – the one on food, which is unsurprising, as ass meat was not a regular food choice during this period.

Max Harris, *Sacred Folly: A New History of the Feast of Fools* (Ithaca, NY: Cornell University Press, 2011); Max Harris, *Christ on a Donkey: Palm Sunday, Triumphal Entries and Blasphemous Pageants* (Leeds: Arc Humanities Press, 2019): Max Harris's two books take the Christian rituals Feast of Fools (*Festum stultorum*) and Christ's Palm Sunday procession into Jerusalem as their respective starting points. The former traces the development of the Feast of Fools and challenges the prevailing view that this ritual was a bowdlerised ritual that attracted censure. Through a close reading of sources, Harris argues that the *Festum stultorum* started as an accepted solemn church ritual to celebrate the subdeacon, only attracting censure in the fifteenth century. His latter book focuses on Christ's triumphal entry into Jerusalem on Palm Sunday. Largely through a series of medieval and early modern examples, Harris exposes the paradox between rulers who usurped the holy ritual to claim authority, and humble Christians who faithfully re-enacted Christ's journey on an ass but were denounced for their attempts to be pious.

BIBLIOGRAPHY

Abelard, Peter, 'Epistola 8', in J.-P. Migne (ed.), *PL*, 178, col. 310.

Adams, Jonathan, and Cordelia Hess, 'Volcanic Archives: Towards a Direct Comparison of Pre-Modern and Modern Forms of Antisemitism', in Jonathan Adams and Cordelia Hess, (eds), *The Medieval Roots of Antisemitism: Continuities and Discontinuities from the Middle Ages to the Present Day* (London: Routledge, 2018), pp. 3–16.

Adolf, Helen, 'The Ass and the Harp', *Speculum*, 25/1 (1950), 49–57.

Ahn, Dongmyung, 'Beastly yet Lofty Burdens: The Donkey and the Subdeacon in the Middle Ages', in Irène Fabry-Tehranch and Anna Russakoff (eds), *L'Humain et l'Animal dans la France Médiévale* (XIIe–XVe s.) (Amsterdam: Rodopi, 2014), pp. 145–60.

Aiken, Pauline, 'The Animal History of Albertus Magnus and Thomas of Cantimpré', *Speculum*, 22/2 (1947), pp. 205–25.

Albert of Aachen, *Historia Ierosolimitana: History of the Journey to Jerusalem*, ed. and tr. Susan B. Edgington (Oxford: Clarendon Press, 2007).

Albertus Magnus, *On Animals: A Medieval Summa Zoologica*, ed. and tr. Kenneth F. Kitchell, Jr., and Irven M. Resnick (Baltimore: Johns Hopkins University Press, 1999).

Alexander, Dominic, *Saints and Animals* (Woodbridge: Boydell Press, 2008).

Alter, Robert, 'Balaam and the Ass', *The Kenyon Review*, 26/4 (2004), 6–32.

Anfindsen, Jens Tomas, 'On Particulars and Universals', HonestThinking.org, available at *http://www.honestthinking. org/en/pub/HT.2005.JTA.Particulars_and_universals.html*, accessed 15 August 2019.

Apuleius, *Metamorphoses* (*The Golden Ass*), ed. and tr. J. Arthur Hanson (Cambridge, MA: Harvard University Press, 2014).

Aquinas, Thomas, *The 'Summa theologica' of St. Thomas Aquinas*, tr. Fathers of the English Dominican Province (Getzville, NY: William S. Hein, 2014).

Arthur, Paul, et al., '"Masseria Quattro Macine" – A Deserted Medieval Village and Its Territory in Southern Apulia: An Interim Report on Field Survey, Excavation and Document Analysis', *Papers of the British School at Rome*, 64 (1996), 181–237.

Badel, Pierre-Yves, *Introduction à la Vie Littéraire du Moyen Age* (Paris: Bordas, 1984).

Barber, Richard (tr.), *Bestiary: Being an English Version of the Bodleian Library, Oxford M.S. Bodley 764* (Woodbridge: Boydell Press, 1993).

Barr, Noel, and P. B. Hickling (illust.), *Ned the Lonely Donkey: A Story for Children* (Loughborough: Wills and Hepworth, 1952).

Baskin, J. R., 'Origen on Balaam: The Dilemma of the Unworthy Prophet', *Vigiliae Christianae*, 37/1 (1983), 22–35.

Baxter, Ian, 'A Donkey (*Equus asinus* L.) Partial Skeleton from a Mid–Late Anglo-Saxon Alluvial Layer at Deans Yard Westminster, London SW1', *Environmental Archaeology*, 7/1 (2002), 89–94.

Bayless, Martha, 'Laughter in a Deadly Context: *Le Sacristain*, *Maldon*, *Troilus*, *Merlin*', in Per Förnegård et al. (eds), *Tears, Sighs and*

Laughter: Expressions of Emotions in the Middle Ages (Stockholm: Kungl, 2017), pp. 153–65.

Bédier, Joseph, *Les Fabliaux: Etudes de Littérature Populaire et d'Histoire Littéraire du Moyen Age* (2nd edn, Emile Bouillon: Paris, 1895).

Beer, Janette, *Beasts of Love: Richard de Fournival's Bestiaire d'amour and a Woman's Response* (Toronto: University of Toronto Press, 2003).

Bellini, Giovanni, St. *Francis in the Desert* (*c.*1480), The Frick Collection, available at *https://www.frick.org/exhibitions/past/2011/bellini*, accessed 15 August 2019.

Bianciotto, Gabriel (ed.), *Bestiaires du Moyen Age* (Paris: Editions Stock, 1980).

Bible, King James Version, available at *https://www.academic-bible.com*, accessed 15 August 2019.

Biller, Peter, 'Intellectuals and the Masses: Oxen and She-asses in the Medieval Church', in John H. Arnold (ed.), *The Oxford Handbook of Medieval Christianity* (Oxford: Oxford University Press, 2014), pp. 323–39.

Billington, Sandra, 'The Cheval Fol of Lyon and Other Asses', in Clifford Davidson (ed.), *Fools and Folly* (Kalamazoo: Medieval Institute Publications, 1996), pp. 9–33.

Boccaccio, Giovanni, *The Decameron of Giovanni Boccaccio*, tr. James M. Rigg (London: Routledge, 1905).

Bodelian Library MS, Bodl. 764 f.44r, available at *https://digital.bodleian.ox.ac.uk/inquire/p/861b32a3-19f7-41e7-961d-e774727708f6*, accessed 11 December 2019.

Boethius, *The Consolation of Philosophy*, tr. Victor Watts (London: Penguin, 1999).

Bökönyi, Sándor, 'The Development of Stockbreeding and Herding in Medieval Europe', in Del Sweeney (ed.), *Agriculture in the*

Middle Ages: *Technology, Practice and Representation* (Philadelphia: University of Philadelphia Press, 1995), pp. 41–61.

Bough, Jill, *Donkey* (London: Reaktion, 2011).

Bough, Jill, 'The Mirror has Two Faces: Contradictory Reflections of Donkeys in Western Literature from Lucius to Balthazar', *Animals*, 1 (2011), 56–68.

Buck, Lawrence P., '"Anatomia Antichristi": Form and Content of the Papal Antichrist', *The Sixteenth Century Journal*, 42/2 (2011), 349–68.

Callan, Terrance, 'Comparison of Humans to Animals in 2 Peter 2, 10b–22', *Biblica*, 90/1 (2009), 101–13.

Caillat, Pierre, and Yan Laborie, 'Approche de l'Alimentation Carnée des Occupants du Castrum d'Auberoche (Dordogne) d'après les Données de l'Archéozoologie', *Archéologie du Midi Médiéval*, 15/16 (1997), 161–77.

Cambridge University Library, MS Li.4.26 f.25r, available at *https://cudl.lib.cam.ac.uk/view/MS-II-00004-00026/77#*, accessed 11 December 2019.

Cantimpratensis, Thomas, *Liber de natura rerum* (New York: Walter de Gruyter, 1973).

Cárdenas-Rotunno, Anthony J., '(Mis)reading the "*Libro de Buen Amor*": Exemplary Ambiguity and Ambiguous Exempla', *Romance Notes*, 52/1 (2012), 3–11.

Chazan, Robert, *The Jews of Medieval Western Christendom, 1000–1500* (Cambridge: Cambridge University Press, 2006).

Clark, John (ed.), *The Medieval Horse and its Equipment c.1150–c.1450* (Woodbridge: Boydell Press, 2004).

Clark, Willene B., *A Medieval Book of Beasts: The Second-Family Bestiary: Commentary, Art, Text and Translation* (Woodbridge: Boydell and Brewer, 2006).

Clavel, Benoit, and Jean-Hervé Yvinec, 'L'Archéozoologie du Moyen Age au Début de la Période Moderne dans la Moitié Nord de la France', in Jean Chapelot (ed.), *Trente Ans d'Archéologie Médiévale en France: Un Bilan pour un Avenir* (Caen: CRAHM, 2010), pp. 71–87.

Cleaver, Laura, *Education in Twelfth-Century Art and Architecture: Images of Learning in Europe, c.*1100–1220 (Woodbridge: Boydell and Brewer, 2016).

Cleaver, Laura, 'Disorder in Nature: The Example of the Ass and Harp in Twelfth-Century Manuscripts', in Laura Cleaver, Kathryn Gerry and Jim Harris (eds), *Art and Nature: Studies in Medieval Art and Architecture* (London: Courtauld Institute of Art, 2009), pp. 131–42.

Clutton-Brock, Juliet, *Horse Power: A History of the Horse and the Donkey in Human Societies* (London: Natural History Museum Publications, 1992).

Clutton-Brock, Juliet, *Animals as Domesticates: A World View through History* (East Lansing: Michigan State University Press, 2012).

Cohn, Norman, *The Pursuit of the Millennium: Revolutionary Millenarians and Mystical Anarchists of the Middle Ages* (New York: Oxford University Press, 1970).

Coldewey, John C., 'Secrets of God's Creatures: Talking Animals in Medieval Drama', *European Medieval Drama*, 3 (2000), 73–99.

Cropp, Glynnis M., and Alison Hanham, 'Richard II from Donkey to Royal Martyr: Perceptions of Eustache Deschamps and Contemporary French Writers', *Parergon*, 24/1 (2007), 101–36.

Curley, Michael J. (ed. and tr.), *Physiologus* (Austin: University of Texas Press, 1979).

Dent, Anthony, *Donkey: The Story of the Ass from East to West* (London: Harrap and Co., 1972).

Dereclenne, Jean-Bernard Y. D., 'Le Prieure de Sainte-Sigolène, lieu-dit Troclar à Lagrave (Tarn): Etude Archéozoologique des Vestiges Osseux des IX–XIIIè siècles (Fouilles 1993–5)' (unpublished PhD thesis, Université Paul-Sabatier de Toulouse, Toulouse, 2001).

Dixon, Thomas, *From Passions to Emotions: The Creation of a Secular Psychological Category* (Cambridge: Cambridge University Press, 2003).

Donovan, L. G., 'Ysengrimus and the Early Roman de Renard', *Canadian Journal of Netherlandic Studies*, 4/1 (1983), 33–8.

Dowling, Tim, 'Pin the Cheque on the Donkey', *The Guardian*, available at *https://www.theguardian.com/society/2003/feb/18/animalrights.fundraising*, accessed 15 August 2019.

Drew, Katherine Fisher, *The Laws of the Salian Franks* (Philadelphia: University of Pennsylvania Press, 1991).

Eden, P. T. (ed. and tr.), *Theobaldi 'Physiologus'* (Leiden: Brill, 1972).

Ehrman, Bart D., and Zlatko Pleše (ed. and tr.), *The Other Gospels: Accounts of Jesus from Outside the New Testament* (New York: Oxford University Press, 2014).

Eisner, Martin G., and Marc D. Schachter, '"Libido Sciendi": Apuleius, Boccaccio, and the Study of the History of Sexuality', *PMLA*, 124/3 (2009), 817–37.

Ernst, Timothy, 'Quidam homo est asinus: The Originality and Influence of Peter Abelard upon Medieval Thought' (unpublished MA thesis, University of Louisville, Louisville, 2011).

Fairman, Tony, 'How the Ass became a Donkey', *English Today*, 40/4 (1994), 29–35.

Faith, Rosamond, 'Farms and Families in Ninth-Century Provence', *Early Medieval Europe*, 18/2 (2010), 175–201.

Forest, V., 'Alimentation Carnée dans le Languedoc Médiéval (Les Témoignages Archéozoologiques des Vertébrés Supérieurs)', *Archéologie du Midi Médiéval*, 15/16 (1997), 141–60.

France, Marie de, *Fables*, ed. and tr. Harriet Spiegel (Toronto: University of Toronto Press, 1987).

Fulcher of Chartres, *Chronicle of the First Crusade*, tr. Martha E. McGinty (Philadelphia: University of Pennsylvania Press, 1941).

Gies, Joseph, and Frances Gies, *Merchants and Moneymen: The Commercial Revolution, 1000–1500* (New York: Crowell, 1972).

Grant, Edward, *God and Reason in the Middle Ages* (New York: Cambridge University Press, 2001).

Greene, Virginie, *Logical Fictions in Medieval Literature and Philosophy* (Cambridge: Cambridge University Press, 2014).

Gregory of Tours, *History of the Franks*, Book X, available at *http://thuleitalia.org/Nordica/Gregory%20of%20Tours%20%20History%20of%20the%20Franks.htm#book*10, accessed 15 August 2019.

Grigson, Caroline, 'Size Matters: Donkeys and Horses in the Prehistory of the Southernmost Levant', *Paléorient*, 38/1–2 (2012), 185–201.

Hammond, Norman, 'Bellini's Ass: A Note on the Frick "St Francis"', *The Burlington Magazine*, 144/1186 (2002), 24–6.

Hanich, Julian, 'Collective Viewing: The Cinema and Affective Audience Interrelations', *Passions in Context: The International Journal for History and Theory of Emotions*, 1 (2010), 1–18.

Harris, Max, Sacred Folly: A *New History of the Feast of Fools* (Ithaca, NY: Cornell University Press, 2011).

Haskins, Charles H., *The Renaissance of the Twelfth Century* (Cambridge, MA: Harvard University Press, 1939).

Haywood, Louise, *Sex, Scandal, and Sermon in Fourteenth-Century Spain: Juan Ruiz's* Libro de Buen Amor (Basingstoke: Palgrave Macmillan, 2008).

Heath, Diane, 'Burnellus Speaks: Beast Books and Beastliness in Late Twelfth-Century Canterbury', *South Atlantic Review*, 81/2 (2016), 33–54.

Hill, Rosalind (ed.), *The Deeds of the Franks and the other Pilgrims to Jerusalem* (Edinburgh: Thomas Nelson and Sons, 1962).

Hobgood-Oster, Laura, *Holy Dogs and Asses: Animals in the Christian Tradition* (Urbana: University of Illinois Press, 2008).

Housman, A. E., 'The Latin for Ass', *The Classical Quarterly*, 24/1 (1930), 11–13.

Hugh of Nonant (Bishop of Coventry), 'The Longchamp Letter', in M. J. Franklin (ed.), *English Episcopal Acta: Coventry and Lichfield 1138–1208* (London: Oxford University Press, for the British Academy, 1998).

Isidore of Seville, *Etymologiarum sive originum libri XX*, annot. W. M. Lindsay, 2 vols (Oxford: Clarendon, 1962).

Isidore of Seville, *The Etymologies of Isidore of Seville*, ed. and tr. Stephen A. Barney et al., with the collaboration of Muriel Hall (Cambridge: Cambridge University Press, 2006).

Jacobs, John C. (ed. and tr.), *The Fables of Odo of Cheriton* (New York: Syracuse University Press, 1985).

Jégou, Laurent, 'La Sépulture de l'Ane. Le Sort Réservé aux Corps des Excommuniés d'après les Sources Ecrites et Archéologiques (IXe–XIe siècles)', in G. Bührer-Thierry and S. Gioanni (eds), *Exclure de la Communauté Chrétienne: Sens et Pratiques Sociales de l'Anathème et de l'Excommunication (IVe–XIIe siècles)* (Turnhout: Brepols, 2015), pp. 197–212.

John of Salisbury, *The Metalogicon of John of Salisbury: A Twelfth-Century Defense of the Verbal and Logical Arts of the Trivium*, tr. Daniel D. McGarry (Berkeley: University of California Press, 1962).

Jordan, James N., *Western Philosophy: From Antiquity to the Middle Ages* (New York: Macmillan, 1987).

Kagay, Donald J., 'The Usatges of Barcelona: The Fundamental Law of Catalonia', *The Library of Iberian Resources Online*, available at *file:///C:/Users/smkl/Downloads/Kagay%20-%20law%20and%20Catalonia.pdf*, accessed 15 August 2019.

Kaye, Sharon M., 'Why the Liberty of Indifference is Worth Wanting: Buridan's Ass, Friendship, and Peter John Olivi', *History of Philosophy Quarterly*, 21/1 (2004), 21–42.

Langdon, John, *Horses, Oxen and Technological Innovation: The Use of Draught Animals in English Farming from 1066 to 1500* (Cambridge: Cambridge University Press, 1986).

Leclercq, Jean, *The Love of Learning and the Desire for God: A Study of Monastic Culture*, tr. Catharine Mirashi (New York: Fordham University Press, 1988).

Leech, Mary E., 'That's Not Funny: Comic Forms, Didactic Purpose, and Physical Injury in Medieval Comic tales', *LATCH*, 1 (2008), 105–7.

Leighton, Albert, *Transport and Communication in Early Medieval Europe* AD 500–1100 (Newton Abbot: David and Charles, 1972).

Lewis, Charlton T., and Charles Short (eds), A *Latin Dictionary* (Oxford: Clarendon Press, 1879; repr. 1958).

Lipsmeyer, Elizabeth, 'Devotion and Decorum: Intention and Quality in Medieval German Sculpture', *Gesta*, 34/1 (1995), 20–7.

Lopez, Robert S., *The Commercial Revolution of the Middle Ages, 950–1350* (Cambridge: Cambridge University Press, 1976).

Lorcin, Marie-Thérèse, *Façons de Sentir et de Penser: Les Fabliaux Français* (Paris: Champion, 1979).

Lubac, Henri de, *Exégèse Médiévale: Les Quatre Sens de L'Ecriture* (Paris: Aubier, 1959).

Mann, Jill, *From Aesop to Reynard: Beast Literature in Medieval Britain* (Oxford: Oxford University Press, 2009).

Mann, Jill (ed. and tr.), *Ysengrimus* (Leiden: Brill, 1987).

Martin, Mary Lou, *The Fables of Marie de France: An English Translation* (Birmingham, AL: Summa Publications, 1984).

Martin, Nancy M., and Joseph Runzo, 'Love', in John Corrigan (ed.), *The Oxford Handbook of Religion and Emotion* (Oxford: Oxford University Press, 2008), pp. 301–32.

McNamer, Sarah, *Affective Meditation and the Invention of Medieval Compassion* (Philadelphia: University of Pennsylvania Press, 2010).

Miller, Nick, 'It Began at the Pub: The Campaign to Shame Brexit's Biggest "Donkeys"', *The Age*, available at *https://www.theage.com.au/world/europe/it-began-at-the-pub-the-campaign-to-shame-brexit-s-biggest-donkeys-20190201-p50uzq.html*, accessed 15 August 2019.

Mitchell, Peter, *The Donkey in Human History: An Archaeological Perspective* (Oxford: Oxford University Press, 2018).

Morton, Jonathan, 'The Book of the World at an Anglo-Norman Court: The Bestiaire de Philippe de Thaon as a Theological Performance', in Laura Ashe, Wendy Scase and David Lawton (eds), *New Medieval Literatures*, 16 (Woodbridge: Boydell and Brewer, 2016), pp. 1–38.

Noomen, Willem, and Nico van den Boogaard (eds), *NRCF*, 10 vols (Assen: Van Gorcum, 1983–98).

Oberman, Heiko A., 'The Stubborn Jews: Timing the Escalation of Antisemitism in Late Medieval Europe', *Leo Baeck Institute Year Book*, 34 (1989), xi–xxv.

Ohly, Friedrich, *Sensus Spiritualis: Studies in Medieval Significance and the Philology of Culture*, ed. Samuel P. Jaffe and tr. Kenneth J. Northcott (Chicago: University of Chicago Press, 2005).

Oxford English Dictionary Online (Oxford: Oxford University Press, 2000–), available at *http://www.oed.com*, accessed 21 August 2019.

Pauphilet, Albert (ed.), *La Queste del Saint Graal* (Paris: Champion, 1949).

Rescher, Nicholas, *Scholastic Meditations* (Washington, DC: Catholic University of America Press, 2005).

Reynolds, Roger E., 'The Subdiaconate as a Sacred and Superior Order', in *Clerics in the Early Middle Ages: Hierarchy and Image*, Variorum Collected Studies Series, CS669 (Aldershot: Ashgate, 1991), IV, pp. 1–39.

Rivers, Theodore John (tr.), *Laws of the Alamans and Bavarians* (Philadelphia: University of Pennsylvania Press, 1977).

Rogers, W. A., 'Deliberations of Congress', The Granger Collection, available at *https://en.wikipedia.org/wiki/File:Deliberations_of_Congress.jpg*, accessed 15 August 2019.

Rollo, David, *Glamorous Sorcery: Magic and Literacy in the High Middle Ages* (Minneapolis: University of Minnesota Press, 2000).

Rosaldo, Michelle Z., 'The Use and Abuse of Anthropology: Reflections on Feminism and Cross-Cultural Understanding', *Signs*, 5/3 (1980), 389–417.

Rossel, Stine, et al., 'Domestication of the Donkey: Timing, Processes, and Indicators', *Proceedings of the National Academy of Sciences of the USA*, 105/10 (2008), 3715–20.

Roy, Bruno, 'La Belle e(s)t la Bête: Aspects du Bestiaire Féminin au Moyen Age', *Etudes Françaises*, 10/3 (1974), 319–34.

Saint Augustine, *The Literal Meaning of Genesis*, tr. John Hammond Taylor (New York: Newman Press, 1982).

Salisbury, Joyce E., *The Beast Within: Animals in the Middle Ages* (New York; Routledge, 1994).

Sasson, Jack M., 'Thoughts of Zimri-Lim', *Biblical Archaeologist*, 47/2 (1984), 118–19.

Scheidegger, Jean R., 'Le Conflit des Langues: Ecriture et Fiction dans l'Ysengrimus', *Canadian Journal of Netherlandic Studies*, 4/1 (1983), 9–17.

Schlegel, Ursula, 'The Christchild as Devotional Image in Medieval Italian Sculpture: A Contribution to Ambrogio Lorenzetti Studies', *The Art Bulletin*, 52/1 (1970), 1–10.

Scott, Alan, 'The Date of the Physiologus', *Vigiliae Christianae*, 52/4 (1998): 430–41.

Scott, Joan W., 'Gender: A Useful Category of Historical Analysis', *The American Historical Review*, 91/5 (1986), 1053–75.

Sheingorn, Pamela (tr.), *The Book of Sainte Foy* (Philadelphia: University of Pennsylvania Press, 1995).

Smarr, Janet Levarie, 'Review of Igor Candido, *Boccaccio Umanista: Studi su Boccaccio e Apuleio* (Ravenna: Longo Editore, 2014)', in *Renaissance Quarterly*, 68/1 (2015), 369–71.

Sobol, Peter G., 'The Shadow of Reason: Explanations of Intelligent Animal Behavior in the Thirteenth Century', in Joyce E. Salisbury (ed.), *The Medieval World of Nature: A Book of Essays* (London, New York: Garland Publishing, 1993), pp. 109–28.

Spade, Paul V. (ed. and tr.), *Five Texts on the Medieval Problem of Universals: Porphyry, Boethius, Abelard, Duns Scotus, Ockham* (Indianapolis: Hackett Publishing, 1994).

Spiegel, Harriet, 'The Male Animal in the Fables of Marie de France', in Clare A. Lees, Thelma Fenster and Jo Ann MacNamara (eds), *Medieval Masculinities: Regarding Men in the Middle Ages* (Minneapolis: University of Minnesota Press, 1994), pp. 111–28.

Sweetenham, Carol, 'What Really Happened to Eurvin de Creel's Donkey? Anecdotes in Sources for the First Crusade', in Marcus Bull and Damien Kempf (eds), *Writing the Early Crusades: Text, Transmission and Memory* (Woodbridge, Suffolk; Rochester, NY: Boydell and Brewer, 2014), pp. 75–88.

Taylor, Nathaniel Lane, 'The Will and Society in Medieval Catalonia and Languedoc, 800–1200' (unpublished PhD thesis, Harvard University, Cambridge, MA, 1995).

Terkla, Dan, and Thomas L. Reed, Jr., "'I'm Gonna Git Medieval on Your Ass": *Pulp Fiction* for the 90s – the 1190s', *Studies in Popular Culture*, 20/1 (1997), 39–52.

Thaün, Philippe de, *Le Bestiaire*, ed. Emmanuel Walberg (Geneva: Slatkine, 1970).

Thaün, Philippe de, *The Bestiary of Philippe de Thaon*, ed. and tr. Thomas Wright (London: n.p., 1841), available at *http://bestiary.ca/etexts/wright1841/bestiary%20of%20philippe%20de%20thaon%20-%20wright%20-%20parallel%20text.pdf*, accessed 15 August 2019.

Throop, Priscilla (tr.), *Hildegard von Bingen's Physica: The Complete English Translation of her Classic Work on Health and Healing* (Rochester, VT: Healing Arts Press, 1998).

Tilley, Maureen A., 'Martyrs, Monks, Insects and Animals', in Joyce E. Salisbury (ed.), *The Medieval World of Nature* (New York: Garland, 1993), pp. 93–107.

Tudebode, Peter, *Historia de Hierosolymitano Itinere*, tr. John H. Hill and Laurita L. Hill (Philadelphia: American Philosophical Society, 1974).

Tully, Paul A. G., and Neil Carr, 'The Oppression of Donkeys in Seaside Tourism,' *International Journal of the Sociology of Leisure*, 3 (2020), 53–70.

Vasvari, Louise O., 'A Tale of "Tailing" in the *Libro de Buen Amor*', *Journal of Interdisciplinary Literary Studies*, 2 (1990), 13–41.

Victorian Refugee Health Network, 'Donkeys can't Fly on Planes – Stories of Survival from South Sudanese Refugee Children Living in Australia', available at *https://refugeehealthnetwork.org.au/donkeys-cant-fly-on-planes-stories-of-survival-from-south-sudanese-refugee-children-living-in-australia/*, accessed 15 August 2019.

Waddell, Helen (tr.), *Beasts and Saints* (London: Constable, 1946).

Wallace, William, 'Albertus Magnus on Suppositional Necessity in the Natural Sciences', in James A. Weisheipel (ed.), *Albertus Magnus and the Sciences: Commemorative Essays* 1980 (Toronto: Pontifical Institute of Mediaeval Studies, 1980), pp. 103–28.

Watson, Thomas Ramey, 'St. Francis' "Brother Ass" and Wyatt's "Ye Old Mule"', *American Notes and Queries*, 19 (1981), 71–2.

Way, Kenneth C., *Donkeys in the Biblical World: Ceremony and Symbol* (Winona Lake, IN: Eisenbrauns, 2011).

Weintraub, Ruth, 'What can we Learn from Buridan's Ass?', *Canadian Journal of Philosophy*, 42/3–4 (2012), 281–302.

White, T. H., *The Book of Beasts: Being a Translation from a Latin Bestiary of the Twelfth Century* (London: Cape, 1969).

Whitehead, Joanna, '"They're Part of the British Seaside Experience, but are Donkey Rides Ethical?", *The Independent*, available at *https://www.independent.co.uk/travel/news-and-advice/donkey-rides-animal-rights-santorini-clevedon-tradition-cruelty-a8483026.html*, accessed 15 August 2019.

William of Auxerre, *Summa aurea*, ed. Jean Ribailler, 4 vols (Paris: CNRS, 1980–7).

William of Ockham, *Quodlibetal Questions*, tr. Alfred J. Freddoso and Francis E. Kelly, 2 vols (New Haven: Yale University Press, 1991).

Workshop of Lucas Cranach the Elder, 'Papal Ass', Staatliche Kunstsammlungen Dresden, available at *https://artsandculture. google.com/asset/papal-ass/fAE79ZFRTcloSQ*, accessed 15 August 2019.

INDEX